11/26/29

ALCOHOLISM

ALCOHOLISM
A TREATMENT MANUAL

Wayne Poley
Gary Lea
Gail Vibe

GARDNER PRESS, INC., New York
Distributed by Halsted Press
Division of John Wiley & Sons, Inc.
New York   Toronto   London   Sydney

Gardner Press, Inc.
19 Union Square West
New York 10003

Distributed solely by the Halsted Press Division
of John Wiley & Sons, Inc., New York

Library of Congress Cataloging in Publication Data

Poley, Wayne.
  Handbook on alcoholism and its treatment.

  1. Alcoholism. 2. Alcohol—Physiological
effect. 3. Alcoholism—Treatment. I. Lea,
Gary, joint author. II. Vibe, Gail, joint
author. III. Title. [DNLM: 1. Alcoholism—
Handbooks. WM274 P765h]
HV5035.P64   362.2'92   78-13435
ISBN 0-470-26523-X

Printed in the United States of America

To our clients

CONTENTS

PREFACE

THIS MANUAL has been developed primarily as a guide for frontline alcoholism workers: counsellors, therapists, educators, physicians, nurses, law enforcement officers, administrators, social workers, and other professionals and paraprofessionals who deal with various aspects of "alcohol-related problems," "alcoholism," and "alcohol abuse" in their day-to-day work. The manual is also intended for use by members of the informed lay public, including clients of alcohol treatment programs, who wish to have more information than is typically provided in pamphlets, yet do not have the time or inclination to wade through detailed textbooks and reference books. It serves to outline our present state of knowledge in the following areas: descriptive or epidemiological information on alcohol use in society to answer such questions as "What is an alcoholic?" and "How many alcoholics are there?" the effects of alcohol on the individual at different levels of functioning, from physiological to psychological "What does alcohol do to people?" theories and data on factors which predispose individuals to alcohol use and abuse, i.e. "What causes alcohol use and alcoholism?" methods which are currently in use for the prevention and treatment of alcoholism and related problems such as "How do we deal with these problems?" areas of active research and investigation which may also provide insight into future developments, for example, "How successful are we?" and "Where do we go from here?"

Given the restriction that the following is written as a manual for frontline workers and their clients, the main objective is limited to outlining the *major* substantive issues and thereby developing a "map" for the reader whereby he will be able to orient himself in the field and be prepared to take the initiative in obtaining more detailed information. For example, we will refer to various drugs which are used in treating alcohol dependency or the symptoms of alcohol withdrawal, but exact dosages of these drugs constitute the kind of detail which the physician can obtain from various sources at his disposal. Similarly, within this manual we will outline major modes of psychologically-based treatment in use with alcoholics such as contracting, thought-stopping, gestalt therapy or group therapy. But the specific techniques involved must be obtained by the professional worker from sources which include more detailed descriptions of these methods and extensive training in their application. To aid the reader in obtaining more detailed information and further training, an Appendix has been included to direct individuals to other sources of information and training-educational centers.

As explained in Chapter 1, references are made to both Canadian and United States statistics and information on alcohol use, although U.S. references are more prevalent. Given the similarity between drinking habits in the two countries, the authors refer to alcoholism as a problem affecting "North American Society." Concomitant with this, the reader will find both Anglicized and Americanized grammatical forms.

ACKNOWLEDGMENTS

THE AUTHORS gratefully acknowledge the Alternatives Program for Alchohol and Drug Dependencies in Vancouver, British Columbia (formerly directed by Mr. Ray Cohen). "Alternatives" brought them together and gave them the opportunity to apply treatment ideas to treatment practice.

They also acknowledge Ms. Margaret Fahlman's assistance in the preparation of the manuscript. Margaret served as Research Assistant, conducted library searches, added some material of her own initiative, made corrections, and typed much of the manuscript.

INTRODUCTION

MILLIONS OF individuals in our society have free access to a potentially dangerous drug—ethanol (beverage alcohol). A substantial number of these people will develop problems as a result of or connected with their use of alcohol. These problems are variously referred to as "alcoholism," "alcohol abuse," "alcohol-related problems," and "alcohol dependency." *The authors do not consider the distinctions among these terms to be of major importance for dealing constructively with the presenting problems.* Far too much attention has previously been given to such matters as trying to decide whether a person really is an "alcoholic." Such efforts may even be counter-productive as individuals fear the stigma of being labelled as alcoholic, with all of the negative connotations implied, and so may avoid contact with treatment agencies.

What is evident to the front-line worker is that (a) individuals present a variety of problems intertwined with the use of alcohol and (b) there are variations in the magnitude of these problems. The term "intertwined" is appropriate because alcoholism may appear to be the cause of a problem (such as depression); it may also be the result of the same problem (depression). Workers in the field of alcoholism deal with a variety of human difficulties such as impaired driving, assault, intrapersonal emotional problems, interpersonal conflicts and disrupted family relations, physical disorders, work-related problems, etc. Fortunately, a variety of disciplines are now trained to deal with different facets of these concerns.

It should also be apparent that the magnitude of the problems may vary. On the one hand we may have a single instance of a "family fight" dealt with by a police officer alone. At the other extreme are individuals whose total well-being from physical to social is grossly disrupted, perhaps irreversibly, by the excessive use of alcohol.

Chapter 1

ALCOHOL IN SOCIETY

ALCOHOL IS OUR MAJOR DRUG PROBLEM

A DRUG may be defined as "any chemical that modifies the function of living tissues resulting in physiologic or behavioural change"[1]. Although we have traditionally not thought of alcohol (or tobacco for that matter) as drugs, the logical framework for a drug must include both of these substances. Moreover, reports such as the Final Report of the Commission of Inquiry into the Non-Medical Use of Drugs [2] have recognized alcohol, along with tobacco as the major drug problems in our society. The report states

> The widespread use of alcohol and tobacco continues to provide the supporting climate for other non-medical drug use. So long as their use continues to spread in all age groups of the population, including adolescence, there is little hope of being able to develop a general climate of restraint with respect to non-medical drug use. The damage caused by alcohol and tobacco is now so well understood that our continued toleration of these forms of non-medical drug use, and our apparent inability to bring about any significant reduction in them, raises profound doubts about our seriousness of purpose with respect to the phenomenon of non-medical drug use as a whole (p. 37).

Irwin [1] has given alcohol a high rating in terms of intrinsic hazard potential and makes an important distinction between alcohol and tobacco in that the potential hazards in the case of tobacco are primarily to the individual user, whereas the hazards in the case of alcohol are both to the individual and to society.

The front-line worker dealing with alcohol use and misuse must be familiar with the information which forms a basis for the above conclusions, if he is to exert the leadership and "helping" functions expected of him in this field. *The general public has yet to assimilate the relative magnitude of alcohol related problems.* This is indicated in the following statement by David Archibald [3], Executive Director of the Addiction Research Foundation of Ontario:

> Three years ago when we reported that almost 20% of our high school students had tried marijuana, parents and school officials reached the edge

1

of panic. A few months ago when we reported that almost 80% of high
school students drank alcohol, and many of them were drinking frequently,
there was one collective yawn. Even worse, there was a feeling of relief that
at last youngsters in our schools had come to their senses and had come back
to something we could all accept (p. 4).

Thus the attitude held by the general public is that because of our
widespread familiarity with alcohol, we can be relaxed about the use of the
drug. This attitude is fraught with danger. It is only in recent years through
a great deal of cost and effort that we have acquired meaningful data on
the *magnitude* of this problem and its multiple manifestations. Most of our
theories of the *causes* of alcohol abuse are theories which were developed
initally to explain other behaviours and have been generalized to alcohol
abuse. They provide useful guidelines at this stage in the development of
our knowledge but we do not yet have a definitive answer concerning the
causes of alcohol misuse. Similarly, most of our approaches in the treatment
of alcohol related problems have been carried over from the treatment of
other behaviours. They, too, provide helpful guidelines for individuals who
are involved in the treatment of alcohol related problems, but we do not
have sufficient information on their relative effectiveness or mechanism of
action.

TAKING A MULTI-DISCIPLINARY APPROACH TO ALCOHOL

Alcohol misuse may be considered as a social problem; a condition
affecting a substantial number of people in ways considered undesirable by
society generally; and about which it is felt that something can be done to
remedy the problem through collective social action [4]. Various disciplines
may try to deal with the problem from this perspective—legislators, law
enforcement personnel, sociologists, etc. Alcohol misuse can also be seen
from the perspective of an individual problem affecting many facets of a
person's life. This perspective will typically be adopted by counsellors,
psychologists and social workers trying to alleviate the multiple problems
connected with alcohol in the life of an individual. Other disciplines such
as nursing and medicine will see alcohol misuse as a medical problem,
destroying physical and mental health. Thus, dealing with alcohol-related
problems is inherently multi-disciplinary in nature. This applies both to the
understanding of the causes of alcohol abuse and to the control and
treatment of these problems. Reference to multi-disciplinary teams and
resource people from a variety of disciplines has almost become a cliché of
modern organizational work, sometimes used to compensate for a lack of
clear directon and objectives. However, in dealing with problems related to
alcohol, the multi-disciplinary approach is essential, this manual will
demonstrate.

It is probably true that the next stage in increasing our effectiveness in dealing with alcohol related problems in society will involve the more efficient coordination of the skills and services of professionals from a variety of disciplines. Dealing with these problems in society involves the combined efforts of sociologists, psychologists, educators, politicians and law enforcement personnel, the medical professions, and other disciplines. Moreover, the recent upsurge of data gathering efforts in this field of study has assisted the appraisal of the effectiveness of programs initiated by different disciplines. Although much more information is required in terms of our information gathering efforts, considerable progress has been made in only a few decades. As Archibald [3] has stated:

> It wasn't very long ago that most of our dialogue concerning alcohol was characterized by two opposite poles: on the one hand, we had the temperance forces intent upon wiping the "moral blight" of alcohol from the face of our society. On the other hand, we had the strong and aggressive alcohol beverage industry demanding the right to market their products with as little interference as possible. There was much ideology, a wealth of emotion, and very little fact (pp. 4-5).

There is still much ideology and emotion attached to this area, but the proportionate contribution of fact is steadily increasing.

The recent impetus for the multi-disciplinary approach to alcohol can be understood in the context of our changing and evolving models for dealing with the problems presented by alcohol within Western society. The early "moralistic" approach saw alcohol misuse as a problem of character, immorality, or defective willpower. The major solutions to the problem to have ensued from this framework appear to involve punitive and legal measures as well as the religious or quasi-religious seeking of help from a Higher Power. Some of these measures are still in evidence, have their legitimate place, and show an associated degree of effectiveness. Although vestiges of the moralistic approach remain, it has been largely replaced by a "disease concept" of alcohol related problems, associated with the use of the term "alcoholism." The disease concept appears to have had the effect of shifting the emphasis in efforts by society to deal with alcohol related problems away from punitive and moralistic approaches toward an emphasis on treatment. Thus, it has been of definite value though not without risks, such as that of suggesting to the individual that by considering himself as afflicted with a disease, he is thereby absolved of responsibility for his own behaviour. Moreover, it must be noted that both the moralistic and disease concepts have in common the characteristic that they do, in fact, go beyond our direct observations and knowledge of the phenomena at hand and involve hypotheses (as yet unproven) about the causes of alcohol misuse on the one hand as due to "moral weakness" and on the other hand as due to an equally unknown "disease process."

The more recently developing multi-disciplinary approach simply starts with the observation that alcohol misuse constitutes a problem to society and to the individual. From there we can approach the problem by attempting to gain further understanding of its causes and using techniques developed by various disciplines and institutions within society for controlling or dealing with alcohol misuse. Of course, the effective use of the multi-disciplinary approach presents a challenge to politicians, administrators, and various front-line workers. The persons working in this field must be willing to relax rigid preconceptions of the essential nature of alcohol related problems which entail "either/or" kinds of thinking. For example, some individuals state that alcohol related problems are medical *rather than* legal problems, and yet we now have data to support the position that certain well designed efforts in social planning derived from legislatively based controls may modify the consumption of alcohol and subsequently alcohol related problems in society. Thus, to fully employ our expanding knowledge from a variety of disciplines, in dealing with alcohol related problems, a certain attitude is required of the modern front-line worker. This involves an open-minded approach to evidence from many sources, an ability and willingness to keep informed of developments in the field of alcohol studies, and the capacity to integrate contributions from other disciplines into one's own area of specialization.

HOW LONG HAS ALCOHOL BEEN WITH US?
A BRIEF HISTORICAL NOTE

Alcohol has probably been with us since the beginnings of civilization. Breweries can be traced back almost 6,000 years to ancient Egypt and Babylonia [5]. Problems relating to the use of alcohol and equivocal attitudes within society toward alcohol also have a long history.

THE IMPORTANCE OF STATISTICS ON ALCOHOL USE

However, it is only in modern society (particularly in recent decades) that we have been able to provide statistical records which describe alcohol consumption in various segments of society as well as alcohol related problems such as accident rates, or medical disorders such as cirrhosis of the liver. By maintaining such records, variations in alcohol usage and related problems may also be connected to other characteristics of society and we may then use these relationships as a basis for inference concerning the causes or control of alcohol related problems. Of course, in establishing such relationships it must be kept in mind that a relationship itself does not point directly to the cause of a phenomenon. For example, a correlation between increased pricing of alcohol and reduced alcohol consumption does not necessarily mean that pricing directly causes variations in alcohol consumption. This is one relationship which can be hypothesized, but others are also a possibility. Other simultaneous legislative or administrative changes, for example, could exert an influence on alcohol consumption. However, establishing such relationships (statistically referred to as correlations) does limit the number of possible hypotheses which can reasonably be formed in connection with a phenomenon and can help to guide us in our understanding and control of this phenomenon.

Statistics relevant to alcohol use are sometimes fragmented and incomplete. Nevertheless, the available statistics are demonstrably useful and must be appreciated in the context of the magnitude of the undertaking and the progress which has been made in this area in only a few decades. The problem facing those who are charged with gathering such statistics is primarily one of being able to command the necessary time and resources for such a great undertaking. To directly assess the incidence of a problem within society requires sampling from the population and gathering data on the individuals who have been sampled. In the case of alcohol or drug related problems it is particularly difficult to obtain the cooperation of individuals in order to obtain information on the relevant behaviours. Thus, we often must rely upon statistics which become available when individuals make themselves particularly "visible" to various social agencies. We can obtain information on individuals who present themselves to clinics for treatment of alcohol related problems or individuals who become visible through medical records concerning death due to diseases which are particularly related to alcohol use, such as cirrhosis of the liver, or through law enforcement agencies when alcohol related accidents become apparent.

The per capita consumption of absolute alcohol yields a very important statistic since this statistic is related to a number of problems for the individual and for society which are associated with alcohol. That is, we do not find a perfect one-to-one relationship between degree of alcohol consumption and alcohol related problems or alcoholism, but there is a definite trend such that *the greater the per capita consumption of absolute alcohol, the greater will be the problems of alcohol dependency, crime, accident rates, and medical disorders related to alcohol.* As has been stated above, statistics on alcohol use are not easily obtained. Edwards [6] gives more detailed information on the problems of epidemiology applied to alcohol.

HOW MANY PEOPLE USE ALCOHOL?

The Final Report of the Commissin of Inquiry into the Non-Medical Use of Drugs [2] estimates that approximately three-quarters of the Canadian population aged 18 and over use alcohol, while one-quarter may be classed as abstainers. In addition, they use a 50% figure, which they consider to be a conservative estimate, for use of alcohol in Canadian adolescents (p. 689). Similar usage patterns are prevalent in the United States according to the First Special Report to the U.S. Congress on Alcohol and Health [7] which classed 77% of the male population and 60% of the female population, age 21 and over, as drinkers in 1965.

HOW MUCH DO PEOPLE DRINK?

Adding up the total of beverage alcohol consumed in a year yields a surprising, if not shocking result. In 1970, for example, each person of drinking age (15+) in the U.S.A. consumed an average of 2.6 gallons of absolute alcohol [7]. This was consumed mostly in beer (27.0 gallons of beer: 1.2 gallons of absolute alcohol); second, in distilled spirits (2.6 gallons of spirits: 1.2 gallons of absolute alcohol) and third, in wine (1.8 gallons of wine; 0.3 gallons of absolute alcohol). If these figures are converted to "standard sized drinks," the average American (and Canadians are close behind)* is consuming slightly more than one drink of beverage alcohol every day.

ALCOHOL CONSUMPTION: MEN AND WOMEN

Ontario data [8] also indicate that there are more female abstainers (25%) compared to male abstainers (14%). The sex difference in the abstainer:user ratio is also reflected in sex differences in problems associated with alcohol use (i.e. more problems for men) although the latter tend to be even more accentuated. For example, U.S. statistics indicate that in terms of quantity of alcohol consumed, men drink three times as much as women [7]. The same U.S. report also indicates that the trend in recent years toward a greater proportion of alcohol users in the general population is substantially due to the increased number of female drinkers. The long term implication of this in terms of alcohol related problems in the population is not yet known. Comparisons of the frequency and nature of problems associated with alcohol in men and women are outlined in Tables 1.1 and 1.2.

It would appear that although this study reports a greater percentage of presenting problems for men than for women in most categories, the

---

* Where Canadian statistics are not available, the reader may make a comparative estimate based on relative population sizes since Canadian-U.S. drinking habits are similar. (Though alcohol consumption and related problems appear to be slightly higher, proportionately, in the U.S., to Canada.)

TABLE 1.1

Specific Problems Associated with Drinking Among Men in Six Age Groups in Percentages
(from Cahalan [21], p. 43)

Higher Scores on Drinking-Related Problems	N=	Age Groups					
		21-29 (104)	30-39 (156)	40-49 (180)	50-59 (143)	60-69 (100)	70-Up (68)
Current Problems Score 7+		25	16	17	13	12	1
Index of Frequent Intoxication		21	16	17	9	9	2
Binge drinking		6	3	3	2	3	—
Symptomatic behavior		19	8	6	10	2	—
Psychological dependence		15	5	12	9	4	—
Problems with spouse, relatives		16	7	8	9	5	—
Problems with friends, neighbors		2	2	1	3	2	—
Problems with job related to drinking		4	3	5	4	1	—
Problems with police or accidents		3	—	1	2	3	—
Health (physician said cut down)		6	5	7	9	4	1
Financial problems related to drinking		3	5	1	3	2	—
Belligerence associated with drinking		12	7	3	4	—	—

TABLE 1.2

Specific Problems Associated with Drinking Among Women in Six Age Groups in Percentages
(from Cahalan [21], p. 43)

Higher Score on Drinking Related Problems		Age Groups					
	N =	21-29 (92)	30-39 (129)	40-49 (157)	50-59 (106)	60-69 (64)	70-Up (60)
Current Problems Score 7+		2	8	7	2	1	—
Index of Frequent Intoxication		2	3	4	3	2	—
Binge drinking		—	1	1	—	1	—
Symptomatic behavior		5	5	4	1	—	—
Psychological dependence		1	4	7	2	—	—
Problems with spouse, relatives		1	3	1	1	—	—
Problems with friends, neighbors		1	—	1	—	—	—
Problems with job related to drinking		1	1	1	—	—	—
Problems with police or accidents		3	5	4	4	2	1
Health (physician said cut down)		3	1	1	—	—	—
Financial problems concerned with drinking		3	1	1	—	1	—
Belligerence associated with drinking		7	3	3	1	—	1

pattern of problems is quite similar. This could provide further clues as to the direction which will be taken by the increasing numbers of female drinkers. *It is a frightening prospect to consider that the incidence of alcohol-related problems in North American society could be almost doubled by projecting the current trend in female drinking habits.* Moreover, in certain populations, women may already have attained the dubious distinction of having closed the "drinking gap." In a survey of the drinking habits of 560 university employees Vibe & Thistle [9] found that women consumed a greater amount of alcohol per occasion than men in nearly every age bracket when weight was accounted for. These findings may be specific to this working population of women as they have not been reported elsewhere. However, the authors conclude that since working women are taking on a traditionally 'male' role of working, along with all of its stresses, obligations and commitments, they may also be adopting similar traditionally male behaviours such as drinking.

It has also been found in a number of countries that currently many more men than women report to clinics for treatment of alcohol related problems. Typical of these reports is an Ontario study of alcoholism in Frontenac County in 1961. Of the individuals classed as alcoholic, 84% were male and 16% were female [8, p. 37]

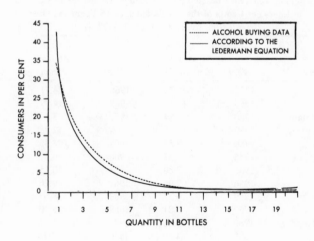

Figure 1.1
Distribution of Alcohol Use in Ontario [from deLint and Schmidt, 1968, p. 972]

DISTRIBUTION OF ALCOHOL USE

The distribution of amount of alcohol use among various individuals in society tends to be continuous. That is, there is no discontinuity in this distribution or natural point at which alcohol use can be labelled as abnormal or excessive (see Figure 1.1). This distribution of alcohol consumption tends to follow a formula developed by Ledermann [10]. It is referred to as a logarithmic normal curve and was proposed by Ledermann following observations of drinking patterns in various countries. The nature of this function is such that the proportion of individuals in various categories of drinking can be predicted by knowing the proportion of moderate drinkers in a population.

CHANGES OVER TIME AND HISTORICAL TRENDS

Historical trends in alcohol consumption in society are also quite revealing. The Final Report of the Commission of Inquiry into the Non-Medical Use of Drugs [2] asserts that alcohol use has been increasing in Canada, particularly among young adults and adolescents (p. 688). They also note that this increase was observable even before the lowering of the drinking

TABLE 1.3

Changes in Apparent Consumption of Absolute Alcohol for 18 Countries in Liters per Capita of the Population aged 15 Years and Over (from Efron, Keller and Gurioli, 1972, [11])

Country	Year	Total Absolute Alcohol	Year	Total Absolute Alcohol	% Change
1. France	1955	25.72	1966	24.71	−3.9
2. Italy	1959	12.17	1969	14.99	+23.2
3. West Germany	1960	8.84	1970	13.49	+52.6
4. Switzerland	1950-55	10.85	1966-69	12.98	+19.6
5. Australia	1958-59	9.57	1969	11.85	+23.8
6. New Zealand	1956	9.37	1966	10.57	+12.8
7. U.S.A.	1961	7.80	1971	10.15	+30.1
8. Belgium	1956	7.96	1967	9.26	+16.3
9. Denmark	1959	5.57	1969	8.67	+55.7
10. Canada	1959	7.01	1969	8.40	+19.8
11. United Kingdom	1960	6.16	1970	7.21	+17.0
12. Sweden	1960	4.80	1970	7.20	+50.0
13. Ireland	1959	4.15	1970	7.06	+70.1
14. Netherlands	1958	3.19	1969	6.94	+117.6
15. Poland	1959	5.58	1970	6.60	+18.3
16. Finland	1959	3.04	1969	5.76	+89.5
17. Norway	1960	3.45	1970	4.73	+37.1
18. Israel	1959	3.68	1970	3.15	−14.4

age in various parts of the country. A parallel trend has been noted by Efron, Keller, & Gurioli [11] in statistics from a variety of countries. These results are presented in Table 1.3. If the slight reduction of alcohol consumption in France is indicative that France has reached its peak ("saturation" point) and if the trends continue in other countries, we may have, in France, a view of the limits of alcohol consumption for Western Industrial countries.

Another interesting historical trend available from U.S. data relates to the proportionate use of distilled spirits and beer. U.S. data are available from the period of 1850 to 1920 and show the proportion of absolute alcohol consumed. Though beer consumption increased dramatically over this period from 1850 to reach a plateau in the present century, the absolute alcohol consumed through the use of distilled spirits tended to decrease. However, the overall consumption of absolute alcohol in the U.S. remained relatively constant over this period [7]. Thus, it appears that the increased consumption of beverage alcohol in the form of beer did not have a net effect of lowering absolute alcohol consumption. This is of relevance to legislators, educators, etc., who sometimes believe that the encouragement of consumption of lower concentration beverage alcohol will lower overall ethanol consumption in the population.

PROHIBITION, LEGAL CONTROLS, AND ALCOHOLISM

As has been noted by investigators such as Klatskin [12] alcohol prohibition in the U.S. brought about a marked decline in deaths due to liver cirrhosis: cirrhosis fatalities rose gradually after prohibition was repealed. The suggestion here is that prohibition may by some criteria been successful, though of course disastrous by others.

The incidence of liver cirrhosis is in itself a valuable statistic. Most of the liver cirrhosis in North American society is attributable to heavy alcohol consumption. Ranking, Schmidt, & Popham [13] have estimated that 65% of liver cirrhosis deaths in Canada are attributed to chronic, heavy alcohol consumption, leading to an estimate of 1,259 alcohol related cirrhosis fatalities in 1971. Furthermore, the incidence of liver cirrhosis across various countries is positively correlated with the per capita consumption of alcohol [14]. Another interesting study from historical perspective was conducted by Seely [15] who found, by studying alcohol consumption in Canada in general for the period 1926 to 1956, and 1929 to 1956 for Ontario in particular, that the correlation between alcohol consumption and death rate from cirrhosis of the liver was .91 for Canada and .96 for Ontario (a perfect correlation is 1.0).

Seely also studied the relationship between price of alcohol as a fraction of the average disposable personal income per adult in society and alcohol consumption and found that these correlations were 0.99 for Canada and

0.96 for Ontario. Thus relatively high prices on beverage alcohol may help to curb the incidence of alcohol related problems.

OTHER DEMOGRAPHIC VARIABLES

Various statistics have also been calculated in comparing different socio-economic, ethnic and national groups. Table 1.3 provides data comparing various countries in per capita consumption of absolute alcohol. It must be noted, again, that there isn't a one-to-one relationship between absolute alcohol consumption in a nation and problems associated with alcohol in that nation, since other factors may modify this association. For example, the First Special Report to the U.S. Congress on Alcohol and Health [7] points out that France, the country ranking the highest in alcohol consumption, has the highest rate of problems. However, Italy, the next ranking country, is relatively low on the problem scale. (This statement must be viewed, of course, in light of data from Table 1.3 indicating that the level of alcohol consumption in France is still much higher than that in Italy.)

Various other demographic characteristics include age, nativity, religion, income, education, occupation, and size of community are relevant to alcohol usage. All of these variables appear to bear some relationship to alcohol consumption. Although any explanation of the relationships would be quite complex, two interrelated factors are very important in explaining the sociological-demographic relationships to alcohol consumption in general: availability of alcohol and the norms of one's social group or community. *Availability* implies the presence or absence of tangible barriers to the use of alcohol including the quantity of alcohol produced by manufacturers, access to vendors, personal disposable income available to purchase alcohol, and restrictions of law enforcement agencies. Group *norms* will be related to the degree to which use of alcohol is sanctioned or prohibited by other members of society who are important to the user, and the presence or absence of adult models of drinking behaviour in the course of socialization of the child.

The influence or potential influence of parental role modelling for drug use generally, has been discussed in research by Smart and Fejer [16]. Results of a representative study on teenage drinking from Bacon [17] are presented in Table 1.4. Alcohol beverages are used substantially by youth of both sexes between ages 14 and 18, although the frequency of use depends upon the State under consideration and upon urban-rural differences.

HOW MANY ALCOHOL-ABUSERS AND ALCOHOLICS ARE THERE?

It has been estimated that ten percent of the drinking population abuses alcohol [18]. This means that approximately *nine million* individuals in the

TABLE 1.4
Frequency of Drinking Beer, Wine and Hard Liquor
Among High School Students, by Percent
(from Bacon [17], p. 45)

	Never	Less than Once a Month	1 to 3 Times a Month	Once a Week or More	No Answer
Both Sexes					
Wisconsin					
Beer (8 oz.)	40	34	18	8	*
Wine (4 oz.)	36	51	11	2	*
Hard Liquor (1 oz.)	56	34	8	1	1
Metropolitan Kansas					
3.2 Beer	56	27	12	5	*
Strong Beer	75	17	5	1	2
Wine	59	34	5	1	1
Hard Liquor	63	28	8	1	*
Nonmetropolitan Kansas					
3.2 Beer	64	25	8	3	*
Strong Beer	85	11	2	1	1
Wine	72	24	3	*	1
Hard Liquor	75	19	4	1	1
New York State					
Beer (8 oz.)	33	30	24	13	0
Wine (4 oz.)	45	40	11	3	*
Hard Liquor (1 oz.)	44	36	16	3	*

* Less than 0.5%.

In this table the figures given represent averages for both boys and girls, and for ages fourteen through eighteen. This means that for boys and for older ages, the percentages would be higher, and for girls and younger ages the percentages would be lower.

United States are to some degree psychologically and/or physically dependent on alcohol to help them negotiate or to avoid intrapersonal, vocational, emotional, sexual, and a variety of other problems.

For the person designated as "alcoholic," we usually mean that this dependency is creating problems for the individual's life on a daily basis a more serious dependency. Jellinek [19], has developed a formula for estimating the number of alcoholics from the number of persons dying from cirrhosis of the liver. Using this method, the number of alcoholics in the United States in 1970 would be 5,400,000: 4,500,000 men and 900,000 women [11].

DEATHS FROM ALCOHOLISM

Statistics from hospitals provide us with data concerning deaths from alcoholism. Death may result from various more specific factors, the more common being connected with damage to the liver or central nervous system. In 1968, 14,600 people were recorded as having died from a variety of such causes connected with alcohol, in the U.S.A. [11].

THE COST OF ALCOHOL-ABUSE AND ALCOHOLISM

There are many ways of considering the cost to society of alcohol-abuse and alcoholism. These costs would include for example, medical payments, counselling services, education programs, lost time from work, traffic accidents, etc. There are, in addition, more indirect and less obvious costs such as the amount of arable land taken out of production for food to supply the needs of the beverage-alcohol industry.

Morris Chafetz [7] former Director of the National Institute on Alcohol Abuse and Alcoholism has stated that in the United States the cost of medical and welfare payments to alcoholic individuals is at least $2 billion per year while the cost of alcohol-related traffic accidents in terms of bodily injury and property damage is at least $1 billion per year. Chafetz also estimates that the cost to industry and workers as a result of lost work time, lowered efficiency and medical expenses, etc., is $10 billion per year.

Some indirect costs of beverage-alcohol include the fact that a great deal of agriculturally productive land is taken out of use for food crops. Thus in the U.S. alone, approximately four million acres are used in the production of alcoholic beverages; on a world scale this totals closr to 20 million acres [20]. That a great number of people could be fed from redirecting the use of this land is obvious.

AMBIVALENCE TOWARD ALCOHOL

Society has, for a long time, held a strikingly ambivalent set of attitudes toward alcohol. On the one hand we recognize the possible hazards associated with this drug, and occasionally go so far as to attempt legally-imposed prohibition. On the other hand, we support a flourishing beverage-alcohol industry and advertise alcoholic beverages in glamorous ways. There is no doubt that for many people, alcoholic beverages carry pleasurable qualities in terms of taste as well as psychological effects. Handling these benefits responsibly, then, is one of the tasks imposed upon a free society.

Politicians who are reputed sometimes as attempting to 'be all things to all people' are caught in the middle of this ambivalence and associated controversy. The following speech is of somewhat obscure origin, but was first recorded during the term of President Buchanan and attributed to "the Senator from Pennsylvania," possibly Thaddeus Stevens:

I had not intended to discuss this controversial issue at this particular time. However, I want you to know that I do not shun a controversy. On the contrary I'll take a stand on any issue at any time, regardless of how radical a controversy it may be. You have asked me how I feel about whiskey. Well, here's how I stand on the question. If, when you say whiskey, you mean that devil's brew, the poision spirit, the bloody monster that defiles innocence, dethrones reason, destroys the home and creates misery, poverty, yes, literally takes the bread from the mouths of little children, if you mean the evil drink that topples the Christian man from the pinnacle of righteous, gracious living and causes him to descend to the pit of degradation, despair, shame and helplessness, then I am certainly against it with all my heart.

But, if when you say whiskey, you mean the oil of conversation, the philosophic wine, the ale consumed when good fellows get together, that puts a song in their hearts and laughter on their lips, the warm glow of contentment in their eyes; if you mean Christmas cheer, if you mean the stimulating drink that puts the spring in an old man's footsteps on a frosty morning, if you mean the drink whose sale puts untold millions of dollars into our treasury which are used to provide tender care for our little crippled children, our blind, our deaf, our dumb, our pitiful aged and infirm, to build highways and hospitals and schools, then certainly I am in favor of it. This is my stand and I will not compromise.

Chapter 2

ALCOHOL AND ITS EFFECTS ON THE INDIVIDUAL

ALCOHOL

ALCOHOL, ETHYL alcohol, and ethanol are all terms used interchangeably to refer to the psychoactive substance of beverage alcohol, chemical composition CH_3CH_2OH. Certain microorganisms, the yeasts, act upon natural vegetable sugars. The breakdown of the sugars is brought about by the action of enzymes (produced by the yeasts), which releases energy to be used by the yeasts and produces a waste product, alcohol. This process is called *fermentation*, and a variety of alcoholic beverages are produced depending upon the original sugar base, that is, wine from fruit juices, beer from malted grains, mead from honey. The yeast action is inhibited by the increasing concentration of alcohol, and fermentation ceases when the concentration reaches approximately 14%.

Alcoholic beverages with a higher concentration are the result of *distillation*. The fermented product is heated and, since alcohol boils at a lower temperature than water, it is evaporated off and collected and condensed in a coil. Ethanol or pure alcohol (concentrated almost to 100%) is distilled by chemists primarily for chemical-industrial use. Different distillates result from the variety of fermented products used—brandy is distilled wine, whisky is distilled from malted grains. Most beverages also contain additives, such as flavourings, or are blended (mixed) from various distillates.

The possible *concentration* of alcohol in a beverage is highly variable and is usually shown as the percentage of alcohol per volume. Beer is the lowest, around 5%; wines range from 9—12.5% and spirits and liqueurs are the strongest, about 40% or higher. The more intoxifying beverages are those containing the higher alcohol concentration per volume. In other words 12 oz. of beer contains approximately the same amount of alcohol as 5 oz. of table wine, 3 oz. port or sherry, or 1½ oz. whisky or liqueur. (Another measurement of alcohol concentration per volume is the 'proof.' In Britain proof equals 57.35% concentration and spirits are rated either under-proof or over-proof. In the United States proof equals twice the alcohol concentration; for example, 80 proof whisky contains 40% alcohol per volume.)

Alcohol, regardless of the form of consumption, is, physiologically, a depressant drug which exerts its major effect upon the central nervous system. The first effects are a numbing of the higher brain centres; since the first centres affected are inhibitory, alcohol's initial effect is stimulatory from the removal of tensions and inhibitions. Projective tests indicate there is also a release of impulsive behaviour. The appetite is stimulated and circulation improved since peripheral blood vessels are dilated. Subjectively, the individual typically experiences warmth, relaxation and a general feeling of well-being and sociability.

Larger amounts of alcohol further depress the entire central nervous system and "although the reticular formation and certain cortical structures have been shown to be particularly sensitive to the effects of alcohol, the depressant effects of high doses are generally diffuse and widespread without sharp differences among areas of the central nervous system" [1]. Judgement, and the related process of discrimination between stimuli are both detrimentally affected followed by motor co-ordination, speech, vision and balance impairment. The most dangerous aspect of alcohol's influence is the fact that as the individual becomes less and less capable of normal functioning, his ability to judge his level of competence has already been impaired. This explains why many individuals under the influence of alcohol express the belief that their performance is either not impaired or is improved.

Higher levels of alcohol blunt pain, cause sedation and finally sleep. Death can result from depression of the breathing mechanism located in the lower brain regions, i.e., the medulla oblongata, but this is rare.

ALCOHOL INGESTION

The circumstances surrounding the actual drinking of an alcoholic beverage are of considerable importance and may assume a major place in treatment efforts. Clinicians, for example, have long been aware of the distinctions between solitary drinkers and social drinkers; between bender drinkers (delta alcoholics) and daily excessive drinkers (gamma alcoholics) [2]. And "gulping" drinks or "sneaking" drinks may be taken as signs of an alcohol-related problem. This description could continue to considerable length. However, it will suffice to stop with the few examples above and establish the following general framework: that the habits or pattern of alcohol ingestion may in some sense be "excessive" (drinking too much or too rapidly) and that they may give clues to other aspects of the person's life or character. Thus the solitary-social continuum may relate to general characteristics of introversion-extraversion. The daily excessive-bender drinker distinction may be determined by employment circumstances or family controls. And a variety of stresses may provide immediate stimulus conditions to precipitate bouts of drinking.

INGESTION TO METABOLISM

Alcohol is absorbed directly from the gastrointestinal tract into the bloodstream. It undergoes no prior enzymatic digestive conversion such as is necessary for the absorption of proteins or fats.

Approximately 20% of ingested alcohol enters the bloodstream from the stomach. The rest is absorbed completely from the small intestine. Other substances ingested along with alcohol can slow the rate of absorption by slowing the rate of entry into the small intestine. Alcohol would normally pass directly and immediately from the stomach to the small intestine but the presence of fats or proteins in the stomach delays the rate of emptying. For this reason eating and drinking produces a more gradual rise in blood alcohol levels than drinking alone, and alcoholic beverages "on an empty stomach" can have a devastating effect on an individual.

Alcohol is essentially a foreign substance to the human body. It is not synthesized (or manufactured) by the tissues as an energy-rich compound, nor can it be stored in any organ or tissue. Very little alcohol can be excreted by either the lungs (1-5%) or by the kidneys into the urine. The only organ that can oxidize (burn off) the alcohol is the liver. This organ contains the enzyme alcohol dehydrogenase (ADH) which is necessary for the initial step of the oxidation process. The enzyme catalyzes the removal of two hydrogen atoms from the ethanol molecule (CH_3CH_2OH) resulting in the acetaldehyde molecule (CH_3CHO). Acetaldehyde is oxidized, primarily by the liver, to form acetic acid and, eventually, carbon dioxide and water, both of which are easily disposed of by the body. This entire conversion process is, however, very slow. An approximate rule of thumb is that a 150 pound man can consume one drink per hour without an accumulation of blood alcohol. The typical drink would consist of $1\frac{1}{2}$ oz. of spirit alcohol, a 5 oz. glass of wine or 12 oz. of beer.

Generally speaking, by virtue of greater body weight (in muscle development, not fat) the larger individual is able to metabolize alcohol somewhat faster. These figures, however, do not apply to all forms of alcohol. Ethyl or beverage alcohol has the fastest rate of oxidation in the liver. Methyl or wood alcohol is oxidized at a much slower rate with the possibility of larger accumulations in the bloodstream causing blindness or death. Denatured alcohol is a deadly poison because of the added toxic substances it contains.

When alcohol ingestion exceeds the liver's capacity for oxidation the level of alcohol circulating freely in the bloodstream begins to rise. This is the blood alcohol level, the standard measurement used to determine the degree of impairment, and is typically recorded as a percentage representing the number of milligrams of alcohol present in 100 millilitres of blood, that is, 80 milligrams of alcohol per 100 millilitres of blood is .08%. (Sometimes the blood alcohol level is shown as milligrams percent, mg%, so the foregoing example would be shown as 80mg%.) The various blood alcohol levels and their associated behavioural effects will be dealt with in further detail later in this chapter.

HOW MUCH CAN YOU DRINK?

Once alcohol has been absorbed by the bloodstream it circulates throughout the body. The concentration is reduced by dilution into the blood and body fluids of each individual. Therefore, an important factor determining the alcohol's concentration (and consequent effects) is the total volume of body water present. This is usually calculated for males as approximately 60% of the total body weight. However this is, for many reasons, only a rough guide. Females typically have a lower percentage of water per total body weight than the 60% figure used, and there is a gradual decrease in this value, for both sexes, with age. Another contributing factor is the body structure of an individual. The above cited figure of 60% of total body weight is based on the amount of water contained by lean body tissue such as muscle. Fat, however, is relatively water free, so the ratio of water to body weight drops in proportion to the amount of fat present.

Although this may seem complicated, basically it means that a light weight person dilutes less alcohol than a heavier built person. So if both individuals consume identical amounts of alcohol in the same period the lighter individual will have a higher alcohol concentration and would register a greater level of impairment on a test. Tables 2.1−2.4 [3] show the blood alcohol concentration (in mg%) that would be reached as a function of time, body weight, and number of drinks. (One drink for the purpose of these tables is the alcohol content contained in 12 oz. beer, 5 oz. wine or ¼ oz. liquor). These tables are useful to guage the number of drinks that can be consumed in a certain time period without reaching a dangerous or illegally impaired driving condition.

Another important indicator of the impact resulting from alcohol ingestion is the outward, behavioural or psychological effect produced by various levels of intoxication. The examples from Table 2.5 are the *average* effects resulting from different blood alcohol levels. Individual reactions, of course, differ greatly, especially if alcohol is being consumed on a regular and frequent basis. However, it is of considerable value for a person to be aware of how he is reacting to different amounts of alcohol. With practice the reader can gauge his own reactions to drinking. This involves a "self-awareness" exercise over the course of various drinking sessions in bars, at parties, etc. The reader is asked to make a mental note of how many drinks he is consuming per hour and to gauge the corresponding effects on his speech, mood, co-ordination, and other functions. Regardless of the number of drinks consumed, though, or blood alcohol level, it is important if a person is going to ingest alcohol (or any other potentially dangerous drug) that he is aware of how it effects him, his relationship to others and his environment, generally.

It is worth noting that an alcohol dependent person may be able to consume large quantities of alcohol without exhibiting the usual signs of intoxication. Such an individual can perform accurately on complex tasks at a blood alcohol level several times as great as would lead to severe disruption of performance in the average person. Speech, motor control and thought processes may not appear to be impaired. The actual blood alcohol level and liver rate of metabolism are approximately the same as the average person, the only difference being that the central nervous system appears to habituate (adapt) to the repeated usage of alcohol. The brain becomes less sensitive to the effects of the circulating alcohol. This adaptation means that larger and larger alcohol levels are necessary to produce a certain intoxicating effect. This phenomenon is labelled *tolerance* and is a physiological-psychological response to the habitual use of any addicting chemical substance, such as nicotine, alcohol or heroin. The fact of tolerance should not be taken by the experienced drinker to mean that he can disregard laws concerning blood alcohol levels and driving, for example, or that he can disregard the effects which alcohol may be producing for him.

Tolerance may continue to increase for many years with the gradual increase in alcohol dependency. A much later stage in alcoholism may occur, however, when the tolerance disappears and a small amount of alcohol is sufficient to produce behavioural evidence of intoxication.

One final word on the consumption level of alcohol. There are many popular misconceptions concerning actions to reduce the degree of intoxication: drinking coffee, taking vitamins, not mixing drinks, or drinking only beer are some examples, none of which have any effect on the absorption of alcohol and the eventual blood alcohol concentration. In order to slow alcohol absorption, food must be present in the stomach. The slower alcohol is ingested, the slower it is absorbed into the bloodstream.

SOME ADVERSE MEDICAL EFFECTS

Alcoholism will eventually lead to medical problems: the damaging effects on the body are the result of a two-fold problem. First there is the direct disruption and the influence of the alcohol itself on numerous body tissues. In small amounts the body is usually capable of regaining normal balance but with chronic alcohol ingestion the affected areas never have a chance to restore themselves and eventually are weakened sufficiently to be considered as in a diseased condition. The second problem, which also causes bodily harm, is the malnutrition commonly found in chronic alcoholics. An estimated 20% of alcoholics show clinical signs of malnutri-

TABLE 2.1
Approximate Blood Alcohol Concentration (mg%) Reached
After One Hour **of Drinking, According to Body Weight**
and Number of Drinks Consumed

Number of Drinks	Body Weight							
	100 / 45	120 / 54	140 / 63	160 / 72	180 / 81	200 / 90	220 / 99	240 lb. / 108 kg.
1	30	30	20	20	20	10	10	0
2	60	50	40	40	30	30	30	20
3	100	80	70	60	50	50	40	40
4	130	100	90	80	70	60	60	50
5	160	130	110	100	90	80	70	70
6	190	160	130	120	110	100	90	80
7	230	190	160	140	130	110	100	90
8	260	220	180	160	140	130	120	110
9	300	250	210	180	160	150	130	120
10	330	280	240	210	180	160	140	130
11	370	310	260	230	200	180	160	150
12	400	340	290	250	220	200	180	160

TABLE 2.2
Approximate Blood Alcohol Concentration (mg%) Reached
After Two Hours **of Drinking, According to Body Weight**
and Number of Drinks Consumed

Number of Drinks	Body Weight							
	100 / 45	120 / 54	140 / 63	160 / 72	180 / 81	200 / 90	220 / 99	240 lb. / 108 kg.
1	10	10	0	0	0	0	0	0
2	40	30	20	10	10	10	0	0
3	80	60	40	30	30	20	20	10
4	110	90	70	60	50	40	30	30
5	150	120	100	80	70	60	50	40
7	220	180	150	120	110	90	80	70
8	250	200	170	150	130	110	100	90
9	280	230	200	170	150	130	110	100
10	320	260	220	190	160	140	130	120
11	360	290	250	210	180	160	150	130
12	390	320	270	230	200	180	160	150

Blood Alcohol Level as a Function of Time, Body Weight

TABLE 2.3
Approximate Blood Alcohol Concentration (mg%) Reached
After Three Hours **of Drinking, According to Body Weight**
and Number of Drinks Consumed

Number of Drinks	Body Weight							
	100 / 45	120 / 54	140 / 63	160 / 72	180 / 81	200 / 90	220 / 99	240 lb. / 108 kg.
2	20	10	10	0	0	0	0	0
3	60	40	30	20	10	10	0	0
4	100	70	60	40	30	30	20	10
5	130	100	80	60	50	40	30	30
6	170	130	110	90	70	60	50	40
7	200	160	130	110	90	80	70	60
8	240	190	160	130	110	90	80	70
9	270	220	180	150	130	110	100	90
10	300	250	210	170	150	130	110	100
11	340	280	230	200	170	150	130	110
12	370	310	260	220	190	170	150	130
13	400	340	280	240	210	180	160	150
14	430	370	310	260	230	200	180	160

TABLE 2.4
Approximate Blood Alcohol Concentration (mg%) Reached
After Four Hours **of Drinking, According to Body Weight**
and Number of Drinks Consumed

Number of Drinks	Body Weight							
	100 / 45	120 / 54	140 / 63	160 / 72	180 / 81	200 / 90	220 / 99	240 lb. / 108 kg.
3	50	30	20	10	0	0	0	0
4	80	60	40	30	20	10	0	0
5	120	90	70	50	40	30	20	10
6	150	120	90	70	60	40	30	20
7	190	150	120	90	80	60	50	40
8	220	170	140	120	90	80	70	60
9	250	200	170	140	110	100	80	70
10	290	230	190	160	130	110	100	80
11	330	260	220	180	150	130	110	100
12	360	290	240	200	170	150	130	110
13	390	320	270	230	190	170	150	130
14	420	350	290	250	210	180	160	140
15	450	380	320	270	230	200	180	160
16	480	410	340	290	250	220	190	170

and Number of Drinks. From Miller & Munoz [3].

TABLE 2.5
Effects of Increased Blood Alcohol Level

Blood Alcohol Level (in percentages)	Average Effects
.02	Reached after approximately one drink; light or moderate drinkers feel some effect, e.g., warmth and relaxation.
.04	Most people feel relaxed, talkative and happy. Skin may flush.
.05	First sizable changes begin to occur. Lightheartedness, giddiness, lowered inhibitions and less control of thoughts may be experienced. Both restraint and judgment are lowered, co-ordination may be slightly altered.
.06	Judgment somewhat impaired; normal ability to make a rational decision about personal capabilities is affected, e.g., concerning driving ability.
.08	Definite impairment of muscle co-ordination and a slower reaction time; driving ability suspect. Sensory feelings of numbness of the cheeks and lips. Hands, arms and legs may tingle and then feel numb. (Legally impaired in Canada and in some States.)
.10	Clumsy; speech may become fuzzy. Clear deterioration of reaction time and muscle control. (Legally drunk in most States.)
.15	Definite impairment of balance and movement. The equivalent of a half-pint of whisky is in the bloodstream.
.20	Motor and emotional control centres measurably affected; slurred speech, staggering, loss of balance and double vision can all be present.
.30	Lack of understanding of what is seen or heard; individual is confused or stuperous. Consciousness may be lost at this level, i.e., individual 'passes out.'
.40	Usually unconscious; skin clammy;
.45	respiration slows and can stop altogether,
.50	death can result.

tion [4]. Malnutrition alone can cause medical problems especially to the heart, liver, brain, and nervous system, organs which require a continuous supply of nutrients.

Alcohol, unlike other drugs, has a high caloric value. For example, 8 oz. beer or 1½ oz. liquor have 105 calories, approximately equivalent to the calories contained in 5 oz. whole milk. However the ethanol calories are "empty" calories. That is, they contain none of the nutritive vitamins, minerals, or amino acids (proteins) required by the body. It is not unusual for an alcoholic to consume sufficient alcohol to represent half the recommended daily caloric requirement (say, one pint of 86-proof spirits) which could result in a diminished appetite for food. Also considerable time, money and energy are expended in obtaining alcohol by such an individual and the routine of meal preparation could be disrupted.

The direct effect of alcohol on the body and the secondary one of malnutrition interact to cause the well-known diseases associated with alcoholism, such as cirrhosis of the liver. Alcohol can also enhance malnutrition by a direct effect on the stomach, pancreas and intestines causing inflammation which in turn impairs digestion and absorption of nutrients into the bloodstream. Malnutrition also lowers the functioning ability of the intestine, therefore exacerbating the effect of alcohol. The ultimate result of such an interaction can be permanent damage to a vital organ, eventually causing death.

One of the top ten causes of death in the United States is *cirrhosis of the liver*, a condition developed by an estimated 10% of alcoholic patients [5]. As mentioned earlier, the liver enzyme alcohol dehydrogenase catalyzes the removal of two hydrogen atoms from ethanol. All body cells must maintain a stable chemical balance to survive. In the liver cells the excess hydrogen atoms from this initial step in the metabolism of alcohol would cause a severe imbalance of the cell's chemistry if not removed. The main mechanism for disposal is the oxidization of the hydrogen to provide energy for the cell. This in itself is not harmful to the cell but it replaces the normal source of fuel, such as the hydrogen from dietary or liver manufactured fat. Consequently the fats (or lipids) accumulate within the liver cells producing a "fatty liver" syndrome, the earliest and usually reversible stage of liver disease. The infiltration of the liver with fat, plus other functional disturbances caused by the presence of alcohol, can lead to the death of liver cells (necrosis). Cell death and the inflammation that may result reduces the ability of the liver to function even further. This liver inflammation is characteristic of alcohol hepatitis and this stage of liver disruption can be severe enough to cause death in 10−30% of patients [6]. The final liver deterioration is the development of scar tissue within the liver (fibrosis). This is the condition referred to as cirrhosis.

Scar tissue is nonfunctional fibrous connective tissue which further interferes with liver function by obstructing the blood circulation throughout the organ. A normal liver removes ammonia (a toxic substance) from the bloodstream and converts it to urea (nontoxic) for the kidneys to dispose of. An ammonia buildup acts on the brain and may cause hepatic coma and death. A second and major cause of death from a cirrhotic liver is the result of the scar tissue obstructing the normal blood flow through the liver. This circulatory block increases the pressure in the portal system (veins bringing blood from the intestines to the liver), causing distention or enlargement in the overloaded veins (varices), characteristically in the esophagus. Death can occur from rupture of the varices causing internal haemorrhaging. It takes approximately 5 to 25 years of heavy drinking to produce cirrhosis, and not all heavy drinkers develop the disease. Incidentally, scar tissue cannot become normal healthy tissue again but some scarring is not necessarily fatal. It is the extent of the blockage of the circulatory system and magnitude of the liver function disruption by the fibrosis that causes death [6].

Excessive alcohol consumption is known by the medical profession to be related to *heart disease* [7]. The mechanics of this are as yet uncertain. One plausible explanation offered is that the accumulation of fats in the liver results in their high secretion rate into the bloodstream producing hyperlipemia (above normal blood fat levels), and this condition is an established major predisposing factor in heart attacks. Fatty infiltrations into heart muscle can cause fibrosis with the resulting disruption of blood supply to the heart muscle. Severe myocardial (heart muscle) disease occurs if the fibrosis increases with a prognosis of eventual cardiac failure.

A nutritional deficiency, especially of thiamine (part of the Vitamin B complex) can also cause a form of heart disease but, more seriously, can lead to progressive damage to the central nervous system with lesions occuring in the brain (particularly in such locations as the thalamus, pons and cerebellum). This physiological damage due to a Vitamin B deficiency is called Wernicke's syndrom and is characterized by anterograde amnesia (a loss of memory for recent events and the inability to learn anything new; old skills however remain unaltered) and an unsteady walk, taking short steps with the feet placed widely apart. There is a psychosis that may develop in some chronic alcoholics that is associated with, but not an inevitable result, of the underlying pattern of brain damage of Wernicke's syndrome. This is Korsakoff's psychosis in which the anterograde amnesia is compensated for by confabulation—filling in the memory gaps with fantastic or extremely improbable experiences. Patients suffering this psychosis lack judgement and are unaware of the implausibility of their stories. The psychosis is usually thought to be irreversible and usually results in admission to a mental hospital [7, pp. 25-26].

The preceding syndromes of liver, heart and brain are the most serious effects of long-term alcohol use. There are other diseases or disorders of the body, either related to alcohol ingestion directly or general debility from poor nutritional habits, that contribute to the general lowering of an alcoholic's expected life span by approximately 10—12 years. The digestive tract suffers if large quantities of straight liquor are consumed, the lining of the stomach can become inflamed (a painful condition called alcohol gastritis), or can become ulcerated (erosion of a section of the lining of the digestive tract). The pancreas can also be affected, become enlarged with functioning disturbed and the possibility of eventually developing diabetes (an inability to regulate the blood sugar level).

Another recurring problem, possibly fatal, is hypoglycemia (low blood sugar levels) which commonly occurs 12—16 hours after high alcohol ingestion, after a drinking bout or "bender." Normal blood glucose levels are maintained by the liver which manufactures glycogen to be stored in body tissue and which is utilized (as glucose) when needed. This regulatory process results in blood sugar levels that fluctuate very little as long as the dietary intake of glucose is adequate. During the metabolism of alcohol by the liver, however, the normal manufacture of glycogen for storage is haltered and blood sugar levels are maintained by utilizing already stored glycogen. A problem arises if the dietary intake for the period preceding drinking has been insufficient resulting in inadequate available glycogen stores. Once the stores are exhausted the blood sugar level will begin to drop. One organ in particular, the brain, is susceptible to hypoglycemia and mental changes (such as confusion or dizziness), with convulsions and coma the manifested symptoms.

The circulatory block caused by a diseased or scarred liver increases the blood pressure, as mentioned earlier, and plasma (blood fluid, not cells) leaks out of the portal system blood vessels. This fluid, together with lymph leakage from the lymphatic vessels accumulates in the abdominal cavity (this is called ascites) and produces the swollen abdomen characteristic of chronic alcoholics.

Alcoholics are also susceptible to pneumonia, bronchitis and tuberculosis, the latter being developed at a rate five times higher than that for the nonalcoholic population [7].

The overall effect of alcohol on the body is negative, and alcoholism contributes to many thousands of deaths annually (see Chapter 1). The majority of illnesses related to alcohol use can be alleviated if alcohol is discontinued or a proper diet administered to achieve maximum liver and other tissue restoration. Permanent damage to nerve cells and liver cells, however, occurs in some cases, particularly with chronic users.

ALCOHOL AND PREGNANCY

Alcohol is carried through the placenta to the unborn fetus. In general, there is no acceptable evidence that *short term* alcohol intoxication or *normal* social drinking by women leads to any abnormalities in their fetus or offspring. However, research in progress suggests that there is a one in three chance of fetal abnormalities in women who drink excessively during pregnancy [8].

In 1973, the "fetal alcohol syndrome" was identified for purposes of medical classification by Kenneth L. Jones and David W. Smith, two University of Washington birth defect specialists. They observed a complex of growth deficiencies, physical malformations, and mental retardation in 11 children of maternal alcoholics [9].

In the five years since the recognition of the fetal alcohol syndrome (FAS) further research has enlarged upon symptomology, and the syndrome is now observed in one-third to one-half of alcoholic mothers. Certain features—such as pre- and post-natal failure to attain normal length and weight, unusually small head circumference, and foreshortened eyelid openings—are found in virtually all instances of FAS. At age one, infants with FAS are, on the average, only 38% normal weight and 65% normal length. Infants with severe cases of the syndrome do not make up the growth deficiencies present at birth even as the chronological age increases. One study, using data from the Collaborative Perinatal Project

of the U.S. National Institute of Neurologic Disease and Stroke found
that 17% of the babies of alcoholic mothers had died within the first week
of life.

Other characteristics which are frequently observed in FAS babies
include mental deficiency, head and facial deformities, joint and limb
abnormalities, cardiac defects, and central nervous system impairment
revealed in tremulousness, a weak grasp, poor eye-hand co-ordination,
hyperactivity, and sleep disturbances. One U.S.S.R. study in 1974 reported
14 of 23 children born to alcoholic mothers were mentally retarded.
Another study, involving 12 infants, showed that all but one had I.Q.s in
the borderline to moderately retarded range. Researcher David W. Smith
reports that *mental deficiency* in varying degrees is the most common index
of fetal damage among the offspring of maternal alcoholics. He states,
"The baby's capabilities are limited, they are limited for life" [9].

While the most recent compelling evidence in support of the fetal alcohol
syndrome has been from human studies, earlier evidence came from animal
studies. Sandor [10] found a similar pattern of deformities and altered
growth in chick embryos as had been observed in human infants; and Tze
and Lee [11] observed that alcohol administered to female rats led to fewer
and smaller litters, as well as offspring that were undersized and generally
shrivelled in appearance. In studies with two different strains of rats at the
University of British Columbia, Chernoff showed that the greater the blood
alcohol concentration, the greater the likelihood of fetal anomalies and
retarded growth. His mice bore defective offspring after consuming the
human equivalent of six drinks a day [12]. Intakes above this level in women
are associated with a FAS risk of approximately 50%. Partial FAS features
have been diagnosed in 19% of babies whose mothers drank an average of
four drinks a day and 11% where maternal consumption averaged only
two to four drinks a day. It was these figures which prompted Dr. Ernest
P. Noble, former Director of the National Institute on Alcohol and
Alcoholism to issue a health caution concerning alcohol use by pregnant
women. He stressed that research has yet to establish safe levels of alcohol
consumption for expectant mothers.

Much is still unknown about the effect of alcohol on fetal development.
It is difficult to separate the effects of poor nutrition, smoking, low
economic status, lack of prenatal care, liver disease, and excessive anxiety
and stress commonly associated with the alcoholic pregnant women from
those effects directly due to alcohol. However, it seems apparent from both
animal and human studies that the risk of fetal damage increases with the
amount of alcohol consumed.

ALCOHOL AND OTHER DRUGS

The liver metabolizes not only alcohol but other drugs such as tranquilizers.
It is also the organ which detoxifies (renders harmless) certain food

additives and insecticides. The alcoholic's liver acquires increased efficiency through adaptation to heavy alcohol consumption. Consequently, when sober, larger than normal doses of tranquilizers, or anaesthetics, are necessary to counteract this efficiency and produce a given effect. However, the opposite is true in an alcohol-intoxicated individual.

This is because at a certain blood alcohol level, the alcohol competes with the other drugs for the metabolic system and the drug dosage would remain active and in the bloodstream for a much longer period than normal. This phenomenon can make prescribing drugs for an alcoholic patient very difficult because of the inability to predict accurately their effect. Tranquilizers and alcohol have an additive or interactive effect on the brain and can cause over-sedation, a problem when an alcoholic hospital admission is aggressive or violent. Even the combination of aspirin and alcohol should be avoided because of their synergic interaction.

The most dangerous drug combination is the mixing of alcohol and a barbiturate, such as Nembutal or Seconal. These two drugs produce similar effects both after ingestion and in withdrawal symptoms, and both are addictive—in fact Brecher states that "the barbiturates might be labeled a 'solid alcohol' and alcohol classed as a 'liquid barbiturate'" [13, p. 252]. When the two drugs are used in combination the possibility of a toxic overdose increases dramatically, since "for either drug, there is only a narrow margin between the maximum dose that an addict can manage and the lethal dose—and it is harder to guage the dose when both drugs are taken together" [13, p. 253].

SOME ADVERSE SOCIAL AND PSYCHOLOGICAL EFFECTS

Crime

Alcohol is highly associated with criminal activity. The Final Report of the Commission of Inquiry into the Non-Medical Use of Drugs states

> Of all drugs used medically or non-medically, alcohol has the strongest and most consistent relationship to crime. In addition to over two and one-half million convictions for offenses directly related to alcohol in Canada every year (including drunkenness offenses; violations of the liquor control laws, such as operating stills, illegal importation and sales; and drunken and impaired driving) many other crimes are also related to alcohol use [14, p. 402].

The Report adds, "There is an abundance of evidence relating alcohol use to more serious crimes. Homicide is strongly correlated with alcohol use" (p. 402); and concludes that alcohol is highly associated with crimes against persons, including sex crimes. For example, the Dominion Bureau of Statistics found that in 1969, of 4,057 males committed to penitentiaries for serious offenses, 29% were judged to also have serious drinking problems. Persons with serious drinking problems were involved in 33% of murders, 38% of attempted murders, 54% of manslaughters, 39% of rapes, 42% of other sexual offenses and 61% of assaults in that same year. A number of studies have also directly implicated the prior use of alcohol in crimes of violence. Data showing that 50% or more of cases of homicide involve the prior use of alcohol are typically reported [15, 16]. Drinking also increases the likelihood of being a homicide victim; two studies reported by Brecher [13, p. 262] found 53% and 69% of the homicide victims had been drinking.

Automobile Accidents

For traffic accidents and traffic fatality rates, The Final Report of the Commission of Inquiry into the Non-Medical Use of Drugs states, "It has been estimated that alcohol related mishaps account for 30% of the severe injuries and at least 50% of the deaths from traffic accidents in the U.S. The Canadian situation is probably not drastically different" [14, p. 395].

Industry

The alcoholic employee is absent approximately two-and-one-half times more often than his nonalcoholic counterpart, an obvious cost to the employer. In addition, general work efficiency usually suffers along with an increased number of accidents and miscalculations. Some companies calculate that 25% of the problem drinker's salary is lost annually. Alcoholism in industry will be given special attention in a later section.

Health

Alcoholics suffer chronic and frequently fatal diseases specifically associated with alcohol. In addition, their susceptibility to disease generally is high and their rate of recovery slow; these two facts combined mean a heavy load of patients for hospital facilities and the medical profession. Exact figures are difficult to obtain because patients are admitted and treated in hospitals not as problem drinkers but as suffering from liver ailments, heart disorders, trauma, etc. Typical estimates for hospital admissions of alcoholics though, range from 10 to 29% of normal admissions [13].

  Suicide is often alcohol-related. One in three suicidal deaths are linked to alcohol with the individual often having high blood alcohol levels at the time of death. In fact alcoholism itself can be seen as a form of slow suicide.

Social

The caseloads of social welfare agencies involved as many as 45% that relate to alcoholism [7]. These cover a broad spectrum of family and individual problems caused by the stresses and difficulties associated with excessive drinking. Perhaps the cruelest results of alcoholism are the consequences suffered by the families that contain an alcoholic member. Alcohol plays a significant role in the "battered child syndrome" and the children of alcoholics have a higher rate of delinquency, crime and emotional disorders than children of nonalcoholic parents. Alcoholism also contributes to marriage breakdown and divorce, and to economic difficulties through loss of work. Families can suffer from a broad range of problems producing a general social maladjustment that requires outside intervention.

Chapter 3

CAUSES OF ALCOHOLISM

THE TITLE of this chapter is "Causes of Alcoholism," not "*The* Cause of Alcoholism." It is not realistic to expect that we will find a single cause of alcoholism, although sometimes researchers, theoreticians and practitioners appear to proceed on this assumption as they champion specific causes which seem of major significance from their experience. From the old moralistic perspective, "weakness of will" would probably be held up as a major cause of alcoholism, while a biological-medical model would look for nutritional deficits or metabolic disorders and a psychologist might try to uncover a "personality disorder." Much closer to providing us with an accurate perspective of how alcoholism develops would be the contemporary multi-disciplinary model: alcoholism is the resultant end-product of a variety of contributing factors, from socio-cultural to biological to psychological. In fact these three sets of factors define the major areas of investigation as we further seek to understand alcoholism.

This chapter will briefly explore the major models or theories which have been invoked to account for alcohol use and abuse. Their significance, however, reaches further than accounting for a single phenomenon since they represent global views of human behavior and will therefore influence any attempts at behavior change or intervention. The front-line worker sees much more than an alcohol dependent person; he also sees a disrupted life style with many facets and interconnections. Thus change, following from models and theories, will be tied to views on the sociological, biological and psychological forces which influence human lives.

SOCIOLOGICAL FACTORS

Is alcohol readily available to a society? Do the values of the society encourage or discourage its consumption, and how? These are two of the major questions which would be dealt with by investigators taking a sociological perspective on alcohol use. As we have seen in our discussion of statistics on alcohol, there is a relationship between economic factors and alcohol consumption. Basically, people will consume more beverage alcohol to the extent that they have money available for it, and this increased consumption in a population will result in a greater incidence of alcohol-related problems. Thus 'availability' is more than a matter of the amount of alcohol produced by the beverage-alcohol industry or the distance a person has to travel to obtain it. The Commission of Inquiry into the Non-Medical Use of Drugs [1] has stated: "Availability ... that is, the opportunity for use and access to a supply of the drug ... remains a primary matter of social concern. Without availability the vulnerability which is created by certain factors of a psychological and social nature would never be tested. Thus, availability remains one of the most important causal factors" (p.33).

The attitudes of a society toward alcohol will be reflected in the customs (or norms) surrounding drinking. For some religious groups, for example, alcohol is strictly forbidden, while for others its use is ritualized. Many individuals in North American society associate alcohol use with special occasions and ceremonies such as marriages, births, and graduations, or with recreational periods such as weekends and holiday seasons. Thus drinking on these occasions will receive the support of peers, while outside these boundaries disapproval, at least in the form of a comment expressing the range from "surprise" to "dismay," may result.

Other sociological analyses may also be relevant to the alcohol intake of a culture. The breakdown of the traditional culture of the North American Indian may be a factor in the alcohol-related problems of that social group. Generally, a marked discrepancy between the goals or ideals of a culture and its ability to achieve those objectives may be seen as a precipitating a factor in alcoholism.

PSYCHOLOGICAL FACTORS

Psychology incorporates a number of different "schools" (a "school" is a general orientation, model, or theoretical framework). Each is usually considered in terms of emphasizing different explanatory principles for similar phenomena—data or observables—although the result of adhering to a particular "school" is often that the phenomena themselves are seen differently. This may have to do with the expectancies generated by the theory.

Psychoanalytic and Gestalt Theory

McCord, McCord, and Gudeman have stated [2, p. 28] that psychoanalytic explanations of the causes of alcohol abuse are based on three major theoretical suppositions:

1. The Freudian view states that alcohol abuse is a result of unconscious tendencies, particularly self-destruction, oral fixation or latent homosexuality;

2. The Adlerian view is that alcohol abuse represents a struggle for power; and

3. A more general psychoanalytic view is that alcohol abuse is the result of an inner conflict between dependency drives and aggressive drives.

Psychoanalytic views hold in common the general belief that the ingestion of alcohol is of symbolic value to the individual. Thus, in order to understand the causes of alcohol abuse, one must understand what it is that alcohol symbolizes. According to the theories, since the individual patient will often not be aware of the symbolic value of alcohol in his own life, it is the role of the therapist to produce, through psychoanalysis, some insight into this symbolism.

Gestalt therapy and its theoretical base may be considered as a merger of psychoanalytic thought and Gestalt theory from the study of perception and phenomenology. This merger was introduced to psychology by Fritz Perls and has found widespread support in North America through its dissemination by the group-therapy movement and in particular, its use as part of the "package" offered in sensitivity-encounter groups. Perls, Hefferline and Goodman [3] in their book *Gestalt Therapy* have described the alcoholic as an "adult suckling," suffering from oral-underdevelopment (pp. 193-194). He is considered as a person who wants his "solutions" to life generally to be in a liquid form, preprepared, so that he can avoid the "excitement" which accompanies the difficult task of grappling with them (symbolizing the difficulty of moving from sucking to biting and chewing).

As Gestalt therapy moves from theory to application, its psychoanalytic kinship becomes secondary to its focus on immediate experience and the fragmentation or wholeness of that experience. Gestalt therapy's major strength lies in its steady insistence that the alcoholic individual make contact with himself and others, assume responsibility for himself and for his abuse of alcohol, and become aware of the self-destructive manipulations and "games" [4] that he plays in order to further the status quo and to avoid genuine behavior change. Gestalt's interest in the "what" and the "how" of the alcoholic's behavior rather than the "why" also inhibits characteristically endless and unproductive historical rummagings which, in the final analysis, serve only as additional excuses for the alcoholic who "can't" begin to control or terminate his use of alcohol. To the professional or paraprofessional experienced in treating alcoholic individuals, these features are most salient and argue for the incorporation of Gestalt techniques into such treatment efforts. They can be illustrated through treatment exercises, which Levitsky and Perls suggest are "experiments that the patient may perform" [5, p. 140].

When clients first begin treatment they are often experiencing considerable feelings of frustration, anger, depression, fear and guilt, among others. The following "games" requiring client sentence completion are designed to help the client bring such feelings into awareness. These games can be used effectively both in dyads and in the "making the rounds" method. The following sentence stems relate to the client's feeling state:

Right now I'm feeling guilt about _____
At this moment I resent _____
I make myself depressed by _____
I frustrate myself by _____
I make myself angry by _____

Other sentence stems relate to the client's abuse of alcohol:

Alcohol helps me to avoid _____
When I am drunk I can _____
If I stop drinking _____
For me, alcohol is _____

Clients participating in these "games" often experience strong feelings about themselves and their abuse of alcohol that they have only been faintly aware of before, if ever. Such feelings may be unpleasant and the client may attempt to keep himself from attending to the feelings and making discoveries related to them. The therapist can help the client to expand his self-awareness by asking that he "stay with" the feeling. This request keeps the client in touch with his feelings and the tactics he may use to avoid them.

Learning and Reinforcement Theory

Learning and reinforcement theory has also been used to explain alcohol consumption. The explanations inherent in this approach are primarily based upon two aspects of alcohol ingestion. First, there is the proposal that alcohol itself has primary reinforcing properties. That is, the chemical effect of alcohol is considered to be tension or drive reducing (relaxing) and therefore reinforces the voluntary act of ingesting the alcohol. A second view is that the ingestion of alcohol may be followed by other reinforcing events or stimuli which serve in turn to reinforce the act of alcohol ingestion. For example, in experimental demonstrations, animals may be induced to drink substantial quantities of alcohol if food or avoidance of electric shock are offered as reinforcement. The human analogy would be that alcohol consumption typically takes place in a social setting where such consumption may be reinforced by a variety of events, particularly aspects of interaction with others.

In any case, learning theory sees alcohol use largely in terms of its effects. If the effects have reward-properties, the future use of alcohol becomes more likely. Of course these reward-properties will not always be obvious. Some of the physiological effects, for example, may be pleasurable to the individual, and yet he lacks the ability to verbalize these subtle or complex states. In fact, in the merger of physiological psychology and the study of fluctuating personality-states ("moods") we find numerous such states which do not have established verbal counterparts in our everyday language [6]. These states may be tied to expressions in body temperature, motor-rigidity, acidity of saliva, rate of respiration, etc. In addition to physiological effects, there are more direct changes in emotions of which the person consuming alcohol may be unaware. These changes may have to do with increasing feelings of power or enhanced sexual energy. Again, these effects may reinforce alcohol ingestion. We should also not ignore the social consequences of drinking. The drinker, rightly or wrongly, may have the perception that his social effectiveness is enhanced—that he is able to control people or that he is more "popular" in a social setting.

Again, we should emphasize that these consequences of drinking may not be obvious to the drinker (or sometimes even to his clinical helper) but that they may have a powerful effect on the ingestion of alcohol. In this context, then, the self-abuse which results from excessive alcohol use may begin to make sense as it is in some sense 'outweighed' by the reward properties of alcohol. As a footnote we could add that there is considerable value in having the clinical helper interact with his client while the latter is intoxicated, should such an opportunity arise.

Predisposing Personality Traits and Individual Differences

Various personality traits and relatively broad and stable behavioural patterns have also been investigated in alcoholic patients to determine whether these traits differentiate alcoholic from nonalcoholic individuals. While numerous factors are found which discriminate between patients and nonpatients, this type of research is poor for suggesting those factors which *predispose* individuals to alcohol dependency. Thus, what we require are longitudinal studies where individuals are followed up for a long period of time prior to developing problems related to alcohol, and the predisposing psychological traits may be correlated with the condition which develops later. This is, of course, very time consuming and costly research. Fortunately, several studies consistent with this approach have been reviewed by Poley [7]. In these studies a common pattern which predisposes individuals to alcohol dependency appears to be a set of traits related to assertive, extroverted and impulsive behaviours. A relationship has not been found between high trait anxiety and the subsequent development of alcoholism.

The trait approach to psychology has been elaborated by Buss and Poley [6] who point out that behaviour is organized in the sense that the likelihood of certain behaviours increases the likelihood of others; that is, a behavioural pattern emerges which is recognizable from situation to situation, and is referred to as a "trait." Patterns which fluctuate to a greater degree from day to day are called "moods" or "states."

Returning to personality predisposition in alcoholism, it has been pointed out by different writers that one of the more recognizable effects of alcohol, especially in men, is an enhanced feeling of power and sometimes overt aggressiveness. Moreover, the effect tends to be greater in individuals who are already functioning high in terms of this trait pattern, thereby multiplying the effect of alcohol for certain individuals. Eventually, then, this effect may lead to alcohol abuse.

For women, on the other hand, some research indicates that social drinking produces enhanced feelings of "womanliness." Wilsnack [8], for example, found that women listed adjectives such as "warm, loving, considerate, expressive, open, pretty, affectionate, sexy and feminine" as a perceived result in themselves of social drinking. The suggestion here is that alcohol dependency may result from the need to have these feelings expressed or magnified and for some women this may be difficult except through the use of alcohol.

Humanistic-Phenomenological Psychology

Humanistic-phenomenological psychologists appear to be relatively less concerned with the formal models of personality than do psychologists of the other "schools" discussed above. Their focus is more on the experiencing human being (phenomenology) and his drive toward self-fulfillment (becoming fully human). Rollo May [9] discusses his approach to interaction with the client in the following manner:

> ...if, as I sit here, I am chiefly thinking of these whys and hows of the way the problem came about, I will have grasped everything except the most important thing of all, the existing person. Indeed, I will have grasped everything except the only real source of data I have, namely, this experiencing human being, this person now emerging, becoming, "building world", as the existential psychologists put it, immediately in this room with me (p. 26).

Analytic, conceptualizing and model-building approaches to personality are then seen as being in danger of losing the richness of human experience. There is also a tendency on the part of humanistic-phenomenological psychologists to think that this awareness-experiencing will develop to its fullest under conditions of acceptance and positive regard from others, while the opposite, negative conditions will thwart development. Ultimately, however, the return to positive growth must be accompanied by facing the negative as well as the positive, "owning" one's feelings and attributes, both negative and positive.

Alcoholism, in the context of humanistic-phenomenological psychology, may be seen as a manifestation of blocked awareness, or thwarted growth. In particular, it is self-destructiveness and may be considered as a result of alienation from oneself and others. Related to this, we could consider the question of lack of integration ("wholeness") in the phenomenological field. "Getting in touch with" oneself and one's surroundings, then, would be required to eradicate the problems.

BIOLOGICAL FACTORS

Another major line of theorizing pertains to biological factors in alcoholism.

Genetic-Environmental Influences

The familial pattern in alcoholism is well established. That is, alcoholics tend to come from families where parents and siblings have a high incidence of alcoholism also. For example, Goodwin, et al. [10] have estimated that on the average, approximately 25% of the fathers and brothers of alcoholics will likewise be alcoholic, compared to an incidence in the general population of from 3% to 5%. Thus, it is not surprising that attempts have been made to determine the degree to which this relationship is governed by genetic factors and the degree to which it is governed by environmental factors. Methodologically, the best designed study for assessing whether there is a significant genetic component in alcoholism is found in the foster child study. That is, if the child is adopted shortly after birth but the biological parents and the child still share a relatively high incidence of alcoholism compared to the correspondence between the foster or adopting parents and the child, we have reasonably good evidence for a genetic influence (barring of coure, pre-natal environmental effects). A study by Roe [11] which is often cited as a foster child study demonstrating no significant genetic component in alcoholism is somewhat weak as a source of evidence for this conclusion primarily because of the small number of subjects involved and their relative young age (28 for control subjects and 32 for experimental subjects). Both factors would appreciably lower the possibility of finding alcoholic biological children of alcoholic parents. In addition, the study is confounded by the fact that more children of the experimental group were placed in rural families. A more recent report by Goodwin, et al. [10] represents a superior study generally and demonstrates significant relationships between biological parent alcoholism and biological child alcoholism. The authors found that 18% of the biological children of an alcoholic would be diagnosed as alcoholic, but only 5% of a control group. The relationships are not expressed to the degree that an alcoholic parent will necessarily produce an alcoholic biological child, but the statistically significant relationship is indicative of a biological-genetic predisposing condition.

Of course, biological factors will interact with environmental conditions. Environmental influences are suggested by the finding of some researchers that alcoholic patients tend to have suffered a higher degree of parental loss in childhood than the average person in the population. Moreover, several studies have demonstrated that later and last birth positions are over-represented in samples of alcoholics from large families [12, p. 734].

Other Biological Factors

Other researchers have focused on aspects of biochemistry of the brain which may be involved in alcohol consumption, although most of this research has to date been conducted with animals [13]. Some chemicals produced in the brain, referred to as neurohormones, are involved in the transmission of neuroimpulses, particularly those related to emotional expression, and may also be related to the consumption of alcohol. Researchers in this area have been able to successfully manipulate alcohol consumption by inducing chemical changes which have also led to changes in the neurohormone content of the brain. Other researchers have directly assayed neurohormone content of the brain and found this to be correlated with alcohol consumption.

Nutrition has also been implicated by some researchers. R.J. Williams [14], for example, is well known for his view that the craving for alcohol essentially represents a craving for a vitamin in which the person is deficient. The role of nutrition in the aetiology of alcoholism is still controversial, though therapies (such as megavitamin therapies) continue to be based on this model, and with associated claims of success.

In summary, we return to our initial statement at the beginning of this chapter: that alcohol abuse in society is the product of multiple causal factors. For a given individual, of course, a single factor may outweigh all others; or different sets of factors may be operative for different persons. Let's consider, in conclusion, a number of simplified case studies which tie in these very broad causal systems or theories.

SOME CASE STUDIES

Person A lives in a "frontier-style" mining community where heavy drinking is the norm. He and his buddies often boast about how much they can "put away" on a Saturday night. Liquor stores provide ready access to alcohol during the day. Numerous bars and lounges are open in the evening and "after hours" there is no shortage of bootleggers around town. This person (and his friends) have had a number of problems connected with the use of alcohol. Fist fights during and after barroom drinking are frequent in town and Person A has his share of cuts and bruises to show for it. He has had one minor automobile accident but managed to settle with the other owner without police intervention. He is a good worker and so far has been able to put in a good appearance at work in spite of being late for work several times as a result of excessive drinking the night before and in spite of working occasionally under the handicap of a "hangover."

Norms, availability and other sociological factors are clearly of great importance in Person A's alcohol-related problems.

Person B is a Metis woman (of North American and White ancestry). Culturally she is not fully accepted either by White society or by the Treaty Indians. She has little formal education or skills to offer; hence she is not readily employable and is constantly living on the border of poverty. Day-to-day life, when not filled with strife or hardship, is just plain dull. Relief from this comes from parties and similar social gatherings which represent excitement, activity, music, dancing, and alcohol. Her use of alcohol, though, is sometimes excessive and has led to quarrels, fights and casual, unsatisfying and exploitive sexual encounters.

Cultural breakdown would be considered as a major consideration in the aetiology of Person B's alcohol-related problems.

Person C is chronically insecure. In fact his insecurity seems to have a long history and can be traced back as far as preschool separation anxieties. As a young child he dreaded new situations, cried intensely when left with a baby sitter or at a day-care centre and accepted school only with great difficulty. As an adult he wants immediate gratification for his needs and finds it very difficult to work through the normal stresses and obstacles which accompany the attainment of worthwhile goals. Alcohol is immediate, pleasurable and provides him with strong feelings of comfort and security. However, he is becoming dependent on alcohol to the extent of damage to his physical health.

Psychoanalytic approaches to the development of Person C's problems would be in order here.

Person D derives considerable social benefit from the use of alcohol—at least in terms of his own perceptions. As he sees it, alcohol relaxes him in social situations, makes him more witty, entertaining and popular. Sometimes, if he has had enough to drink, he can even become "the life of the party." Of course he often overdoes it; drinking bouts lead more and more to sessions of vomiting in the bathroom. And the parties he attends, the people he associates with are becoming more selective. His friends are now more limited to heavy drinkers like himself.

Learning theory would be particularly relevant here in examining the reinforcing value of alcohol.

Person E feels insecure with men. She is generally unsure of her femininity. As a rule she is rather controlled, precise and is a perfectionist. Some of her friends consider her to be compulsive in various habits such as housekeeping and personal grooming. This personality pattern is rather marked and stands out from the way her friends appear to be. However, having had a few drinks, she opens up and feels sexy and attractive at social gatherings or when on dates. Unfortunately these "good feelings" seldom occur when she is not drinking.

For this person, personality predisposition should be examined as a major contributor to alcohol use.

Person F is a hard-working late-middle-aged businessman. After a childhood marked by financial hardship for his family, he worked his way through business college with a firm "pull yourself up by your own bootstraps" philosophy. At this stage of his life, he has most of the material possessions he could want. Yet he is left with a vague sense of dissatisfaction about his achievement and his relations with others. Somehow, more struggling "up the organization" doesn't quite make sense but he does not know where to turn. His drinking at business luncheons, after work, and in the evenings is becoming excessive.

For Person F, self-actualization, and its particular meaning for him would bear examining.

Person G has not had particularly disruptive, traumatic or frustrating circumstances in his life—with the exception of those caused by his excessive use of alcohol. Overall, it is difficult to find a factor, either within his personality or in his environment, which could have caused his current problems with alcohol. However, one clue is provided by his mother's report that from a very early age he seemed to have a strong predilection for beverage alcohol. As a preschooler, he would sneak sips of drinks at adult parties: not that unusual, perhaps, but it did seem a little excessive at times. A few years later, he was occasionally discovered stealing drinks from his parent's liquor supply. And adolescent alcohol use with peers started early and quickly become excessive.

For Person G the various biological factors could be considered as having aetiological significance.

Chapter 4

BROAD SPECTRUM TREATMENT PROGRAMS

THIS CHAPTER deals with some of the more significant broad-based treatment programs. Within each of these programs, more specific "schools" of therapy or treatment interventions are introduced. These will be discussed in subsequent chapters.

INPATIENT VERSUS OUTPATIENT TREATMENT

Alcohol dependent individuals may be treated as inpatients in hospitals and halfway house settings or as outpatients in community mental health agencies and alcohol clinics. Inpatient care is much more expensive than outpatient care and represents a greater disruption to the client and the client's family. While more controlled research is required on the issue of the relative effectiveness of inpatient versus outpatient treatment, available studies suggest that prolonged inpatient treatment does not facilitate better treatment outcome than outpatient treatment; furthermore the nature of treatment rendered may interact with the type of client treated [1].

Edwards [2] and Edwards and Guthrie [3, 4] found that an average of nearly eight weeks of "intensive" outpatient care followed by less intensive outpatient aftercare was more effective than an average of nearly nine weeks of inpatient treatment followed by outpatient aftercare. Treatment effectiveness was evaluated with regard to global ratings over 12 months following intensive treatment. In a study of chronic municipal court offenders, Gallant [5] found no significant differences on a variety of outcome measures for those involuntarily placed in one month of inpatient treatment followed by five months of coerced outpatient treatment compared with those involuntarily placed in six months of outpatient treatment. Wanberg, Horn, and Fairchild [6] found two weeks of intensive inpatient treatment followed by outpatient group therapy to be more effective at a three month follow-up (after intake) than three or more in-community treatment sessions followed by outpatient group therapy. Though the Wanberg et al. [6] effects contradict those of Edwards [2] and Edwards and Guthrie [3, 4], it should be noted that the length of both intensive treatment and evaluation were considerably different in the two studies, being several times longer in the latter study, and that the effects found by Wanberg et al. [6] were short-term. The above studies suggest then that inpatient treatment does not appear to enhance the likelihood of long-term treatment success and that, apart from short-term medical considerations for more seriously deteriorated alcoholics, less expensive outpatient programs may serve the alcoholic in treatment as well as inpatient programs.

EFFECTIVENESS OF INPATIENT AND OUTPATIENT TREATMENT

In a review of 30 inpatient studies, Baekeland et al. [7] report that 41.5% of the clients, on average, appear to improve as a result of treatment. Eighteen outpatient clinics reported, on average, an improvement rate of 41.6%, virtually the same improvement rate for inpatient care. The authors point out that these improvement rates would likely drop around 5% if spontaneous (nontreatment related) improvement is taken into account.

WHICH CLIENTS DO BETTER?

It has been found, in both inpatient and outpatient outcome studies, that certain clients tend to do better in treatment than others. Positive treatment outcome is associated with marital and occupation stability, higher socioeconomic status, higher I.Q. and better education, social skill, later onset of heavy drinking, no court convictions, fewer prior treatment involvements, level of motivation, and length of abstinence in the year prior to treatment. Conversely, negative outcome is associated with lower socioeconomic class, social isolation, occupational and marital instability, poor motivation, history of dropping out of treatment, severity of illness, arrest history, and psychopathology [8,9].

Gibbs and Flanagan [10] in a review of 45 studies attempted to isolate the characteristics of alcoholics generally associated with positive therapy outcome. Though they did not discover stable predictors across all studies they found that some personal characteristics tended to be of more predictive value than others. Congruent with the Baekeland [8] and Emrick [9] findings, reasonably consistent positive predictors were found to include stable work history, stable marital relationship, high status occupation, high level of motivation, and a longer period of abstinence prior to admission. Other positive predictors include a willingness to take disulfiram, no history of delirium tremens, diagnosis of psychoneurosis, low PD (Psychopathic Deviate) scale score on the MMPI, and high Arithmetic score on the Wechsler Adult Intelligence Scale. Drinking history indicators were not found to be predictive of treatment outcome and, unlike the studies cited in Baekeland's review [8], Gibbs and Flanagan [10] found age at admission, intelligence, level of education, and arrest history to be uncertain predictors of treatment outcome—of predictive value in some studies but not of predictive value in a significant number of other studies.

Workers* in the field of alcoholism are all aware of the likelihood of many individuals dropping out of treatment or, indeed, not engaging in treatment in the first place. Inpatient dropout rates range from 13—40% with a mean of 28%. Outpatient dropout rates tend to be higher, ranging from 52—75% of patients by the fourth session [7]. Since dropouts benefit less from treatment than those who continue [11] it is important to take steps to enhance the likelihood of the patient continuing in treatment. Such measures as immediate needs counseling (for housing or social assistance for example), using group rather than individual intake session [12] and follow-up contact by phone or mail with clients who miss appointments [13] appear to help in keeping such clients in treatment.

The "personal touch" appears to also enhance the likelihood of a successful referral (by "successful referral" we mean that the client will make contact with the agency to which he is referred) from a hospital or detoxification centre to the community mental health agency or alcohol clinic. Chafetz et al. [14, 15] found that simply having the patient seen by a psychiatrist and social worker boosted the rate of successful referrals to 65% from the usual 5%. Likewise, a visit by a social worker to female alcoholics in a correctional setting increased the successful referral rate to 59% from 1% [16]. Writing or telephoning the patient to remind him about the first appointment also increases the chances of a successful referral [17, 18].

Negative factors at the time of referral may contribute to the person not following through on the first appointment. Perceived anger in the voice of the referring party or delay in scheduling the initial appointment contribute to dropping out at the referral stage [19, 20]. Clearly it is important for all workers to convey to the patient satisfactory levels of acceptance and regard (that mental health workers are sometimes negatively disposed to their alcoholic patients or clients has been reported [21]).

DETOXIFICATION PROGRAMS

One of the first considerations in the treatment of alcohol abuse is the supervision of the patient's withdrawal from alcohol. Such withdrawals are generally managed either in hospital chemical dependency units or detoxification facilities designed primarily for alcohol abusers.

Patients are typically brought to such facilities by friends, relatives,

---

* The term "workers" is used to include all those involved in the medical, social, and psychological rehabilitation of alcoholic individuals whether at professional, paraprofessional, or lay levels.

alcohol workers, or the police. At times they arrive unassisted. Residence in the detoxification facilities lasts usually from 2—5 days, even up to two weeks in some cases. Usually about half of the admissions simply require time to sober up, the other half may need brief treatment for mild to moderate withdrawal. Those experiencing delirium tremens (the "D.T.s") or withdrawal seizures (about half of all individuals withdrawing) may be transferred to a hospital. The possibility of death occurring as a complication of withdrawal is serious, particularly when untreated.

An excellent description of the clinical manifestations of the phases of alcohol withdrawal as well as their treatment may be found in Victor & Wolfe [22]. It is important to note that minor withdrawal usually occurs within the first 48 hours after cessation of drinking and is described by Victor & Wolfe (1973) as "essentially benign." Major withdrawal (delirium tremens) occurs later and ends fatally in about 15% of cases.

Most patients are beginning to experience withdrawal symptoms by the time they arrive at the detoxification facility. Such symptoms typically begin to occur a few hours after the last drink. The severity of the withdrawal symptoms cannot be predicted by the amount of alcohol consumed or duration of drinking. In order of increasing severity, the symptoms may include:

- Acute tremulousness
- Tremor and transitory hallucinations
- Acute auditory hallucinations
- Epilepsy rum fits
- Typical delirium tremens
- Atypical delirium tremens

The following considerations typically constitute clinical treatment of withdrawal:

1. A general history is taken, and alcoholic complications as well as non-alcoholic complications are noted;

2. Basic vital signs are recorded every four hours until the patient is no longer in danger;

3. In the case of overhydration, diuretic therapy is instituted;

4. In the case of dehydration, frequent small amounts of oral fluids are given, depending on the extent of dehydration;

5. Diets are supplemented with bedtime feedings and milk and fruit juices between meals;

6. Daily dosages of Vitamin B complex and Vitamin C are given;

7 Minor tranquilizers, usually Librium or Valium are given. The dosage and type of tranquilizer are dictated by the severity of autonomic overactivity and anxiety, and the particular needs of the patient. Tranquilizers are used to prevent withdrawal seizures. The most frequently used anticonvul-

sant drug for alcohol abuse has been diphenylhydantoin (Dilantin). Dilantin's effect however is so delayed that it does not prevent withdrawal seizures during the early stages of alcohol withdrawal.

8. Hypomagnesia may occur among those alcoholics whose nutrition has been neglected. While some physicians routinely administer magnesium, others will do so only to those demonstrating poor nutrition. Still others may administer it only if low serum magnesium is indicated by laboratory analysis.

Patients admitted to detoxification facilities often present associated medical complications. It is important that all such patients receive immediate and comprehensive evaluation of their health problems. For detailed material the reader is referred to reports by Victor [23] and Knott and Beard [24] describing the medical concerns involved in the withdrawal treatment of alcoholism.

It is not uncommon for detoxification facilities to be abused by those they are designed to serve. Some patients regard such facilities as convenient places to sober up in order to return to abusive drinking upon discharge. This "revolving door" pattern is demoralizing for the detoxification staff, is wasteful of community funds, and, above all, is a disservice to the patients who are motivated to improve their condition. This phenomenon serves to illustrate the importance of addressing the patient's abuse of alcohol from as broad a base as possible. Physical withdrawal from alcohol is a necessary approach to the successful rehabilitation of the alcoholic patient, but insufficient of itself.

ALCOHOLICS ANONYMOUS

Alcoholics Anonymous (A.A.) is a self-help organization founded in the United States in 1935 by two alcoholics, Bill W. and Dr. Bob, for the express purpose of providing a fellowship for compulsive drinkers desiring to abstain from alcohol. Over the past four decades A.A. has become a world-wide organization with over 16,000 autonomous groups in the United States and Canada and 12,000 groups in over 90 other countries around the world. With contributing membership in the United States at an estimated 320,000 in 1976 [25], A.A. reaches about 4% of the alcoholic population, nearly as many as does the medical profession, either private practitioners or medical personnel in psychiatric facilities [7].

A.A. is an integral part of most inpatient and many outpatient programs. Members are urged to attend at least one meeting per week. The primary function of the meetings is to share personal narratives concerning the severe problems which alcohol posed in the past to the member's health, job, family, finances, etc., and to explain how the A.A. program helped them achieve and maintain sobriety. Sharing of such personal histories with other self-confessed alcoholics strengthens the bonds between them and provides, for many of its participants, the first genuine circle of friends.

In A.A. meetings, psychological traits characteristic of alcoholics are confronted, while their opposite traits are fostered. Thus, denial is replaced by frank and open acknowledgment of one's problems with alcohol. Self-responsibility takes the place of resentment and blaming of others for one's own problems. Though the A.A. process is unstructured, it is guided by the philosophy outlined in the "Twelve Steps." The Twelve Steps are as follows:

1. We admitted we were powerless over alcohol—that our lives had become unmanageable.

2. We came to believe that a Power greater than ourselves could restore us to sanity.

3. We made a decision to turn our will and our lives over to the care of God as we understood Him.

4. We made a searching and fearless moral inventory of ourselves.

5. We admitted to God, to ourselves, and to another human being the exact nature of our wrongs.

6. We were entirely ready to have God remove all these defects of character.

7. We humbly asked Him to remove our shortcomings.

8. We made a list of all persons we had harmed and became willing to make amends to them all.

9. We directed amends to such people wherever possible, except when to do so would injure them or others.

10. We continued to take personal inventory and when we were wrong promptly admitted it.

11. We sought through prayer and meditation to improve our conscious contact with God, as we understood him, praying only for knowledge of His Will for us and the power to carry that out.

12. Having had a spiritual awakening as the result of these steps we tried to carry this message to alcoholics and practice these principles in all our affairs.

WHAT KIND OF PEOPLE ATTEND ALCOHOLICS ANONYMOUS?

A relatively small percentage (3.5%) of alcohol dependent individuals actively participate in A.A. meetings. Successful A.A. members are likely to have lost their drinking friends, to be socially and verbally skilled, and to have had no close friend or relative who had quit drinking on their own. Though not class conscious they tend to come from lower-middle to upper middle socioeconomic levels; few skid row persons participate in A.A.[26].

Those who do not often participate in or succeed in A.A. include chronic skid-row alcoholics, those who are not socially or verbally skilled or those who reject the implicit religious orientation. Others are uncomfortable with presenting self-depreciating personal narratives which they feel are "no one else's business" and are skeptical of the tendency inherent in such a process to exaggerate and embellish the report of the depths to which the narrator sunk, a sort of alcoholic "one upmanship." Still others are not prepared to abstain nor do they define themselves so readily as "alcoholics."

 ## DO THEY SUCCEED?

Objective data on A.A.s effectiveness are hard to come by. A.A. has not always cooperated with those interested in researching its effectiveness. What little data does exist suggests that A.A. is not nearly as effective as many workers in the field believe. Rather than a 75% improvement rate at one year [27, 28] or the 60% reported by A.A. itself [29], the only hard data on A.A.'s effectiveness [30] suggest that 34.6% of A.A. members are abstinent at the end of one year. Since the data cover only those who attended at least ten times and A.A. does not attract chronic skid row alcoholics, A.A.'s success rate does not appear as impressive as many in the field believe it to be. The above figure of 34.6% is supported by Ditman's [31] estimate of a 30–35% "cure" rate for A.A. members. Thus A.A.'s success would appear to be in the same range as the success of outpatient and inpatient programs.

A.A. groups may be found listed in the telephone directory of virtually every city of any size across the United States and Canada and can be counted on to extend their services generously to the alcoholic newcomer and/or his family. The interested reader is referred to the A.A. "Big Book" now in its third edition [32], the monthly *A.A. Grapevine,* and other A.A. pamphlets, bulletins and directories for additional information. Detailed information concerning the development, growth, size, assumptions, effectiveness, and literature of A.A. is reported in Leach and Norris [33].

 ## DRINKWATCHERS

Drinkwatchers (DW) is a three-year-old nonprofit "educational organization of self-help and supportive therapy dedicated to help prevent and overcome problems with alcohol" [34]. An alternative to the required abstinence of A.A., Drinkwatchers offers its members a choice of drinking goals—abstinence or controlled drinking. DW characteristically refers chronic alcoholics who have no apparent ability to control their drinking to A.A. type programs or to detoxification facilities. As such, DW does not see itself conflicting with programs that already exist.

Drinkwatchers appears more inclined to avail itself of recent developments in nutritional and therapeutic approaches to the abuse of alcohol. It emphasizes sound nutrition and draws from rational-emotive and behavioral approaches to facilitate controlled drinking, or abstinence, on the part of its members. Drinkwatchers has not been in operation long enough to generate outcome statistics. Nonetheless, given its openness to current research on the treatment of alcoholism, it is expected that DW will make itself available to outside objective assessment of its effectiveness.

To date, more than 50 autonomous, self-supporting DW groups have been organized in the United States, Canada, and Mexico. Frequently led by a professional volunteering his or her time, the groups invite speakers or have discussions on limiting alcohol use. Only nonalcoholic beverages are served in the meetings; individuals who arrive at the meetings intoxicated are asked to leave.

More on DW and its philosophy is available in a book by its founder and director, Ms. Ariel Winters entitled *How To Be A Drinkwatcher.* Parallel views may be found in *Drink to Your Health* by Junius Adams [35] and *Why Drinking Can Be Good For You* by Morris Chafetz. These books and materials on DW are available from Drinkwatchers, P.O. Box 179, Haverstraw, New York, 10927.

CONTROLLED DRINKING IN GENERAL

Traditional approaches to the problem of alcohol abuse have had as their goal, with rare exception, complete and total abstinence from alcohol. This view of alcoholism derives from the "disease model" of alcoholism which proposes that alcoholics suffer from a progressive and irreversible disorder. It is expected that such individuals will necessarily drink to the point of intoxication after consuming even small amounts of alcohol.

Investigations over the past decade have failed to support the loss of control thesis [36, 37, 38] or the idea that alcoholic individuals never become controlled drinkers [39, 40]. In other studies, clinicians using principles developed by research psychologists have successfully taught chronic alcoholics to drink socially. At this point, then, it seems that the burden of proof rests with those adhering to the increasingly doubtful "disease model" of alcoholism.

In recent years a number of experimental studies have demonstrated the viability of controlled drinking as a treatment option for some individuals who have come to abuse alcohol. Although research on the type of individuals who are appropriate for controlled drinking remains to be done, clinical evidence to date suggests that the following types of individuals may be appropriate candidates:

1. Those who have successfully practiced social drinking in the past and do not identify themselves as alcoholics;
2. Those with stable marital and vocational histories;
3. Those who have environmental support for controlled drinking;
4. Those who prefer the controlled drinking option over abstinence; and
5. Those whose family histories evidence little or no alcoholism.

A variety of treatment approaches designed to inculcate controlled drinking in individuals who abuse alcohol have been recently investigated. Lovibond and Caddy [41, 42] trained alcoholics to discriminate their own blood alcohol levels and then to use the discriminations to keep their alcohol consumption within reasonable limits. Other studies [43, 44] have supported the feasibility of blood alcohol concentration training. In a more experimental vein, Cohen and her colleagues [45, 46, 47, 48, 49] have altered the alcohol consumption of alcoholic inpatients by manipulating the consequences of excessive drinking. Sobell and his colleagues [50, 51, 52, 53] have explored the impact of a broad-based behavioural approach (aversive conditioning, social skills training, drink refusal practice, videotape replay, stimulus control training) on the excessive drinking of their inpatients. During months 19−24 following treatment, controlled clients spent 87% of their days free, with moderate or no alcohol consumption. Subjects in a comparison group spent only 44% of their days free, with moderate or no alcohol consumption. Parallel data for experimental abstinence clients was 66% and 46% for control clients. These data reflect high rate of improvement but also generate questions. What, for example, were the active components of the program? Why did experimental controlled drinking clients *abstain* as frequently (64% of their days) as experimental abstinence clients (62% of their days)?

Even though the series of studies by Sobell and his colleagues raise some questions it seems clear that broad spectrum, multi-faceted treatment programs aimed at the "whole" person will be more effective than treatment efforts directed at the problem drinking alone [54, 55, 56, 57]. Such broad spectrum treatment approaches to controlled drinking would likely be based on:

1. Investigation of situation, feelings or thoughts that occur before, during and after excessive drinking;
2. Arranging effective alternative responses to excessive drinking;
3. Learning how controlled drinking differs from alcoholic drinking and practicing controlled drinking while under observation;
4. Practicing drink refusal; and
5. Establishing contracts with the treatment agency and/or spouse to reward periods of controlled drinking and to levy penalties (i.e., loss of attention and monetary fines) for excessive drinking.

In conclusion, the available data suggest that *some* alcoholics can, with adequate training, successfully adopt controlled drinking patterns. Certain precautions must be noted, however. The most important is that *not all* alcoholics have successfully engaged in controlled drinking following treatment. No guarantees exist for the alcoholic undergoing treatment designed to facilitate a return to controlled drinking. Moreover, it is not known with any degree of certainty *which* alcoholic individuals can be expected to successfully benefit from such treatment.

The final precaution concerns the type of treatment the alcoholic enters into to achieve controlled drinking. A variety of treatment approaches have been employed in the past to address the problem of alcoholism. They enjoy varying rates of success. Of these approaches, behaviour therapy has taken the lead in the research on controlled drinking and has contributed the most to the development of treatment approaches for the alcoholic individual desiring to return to social drinking. It is expected that treatment outcome will be enhanced when the therapist is familiar with and employs behavioural principles to moderate the alcoholic's drinking patterns.

The subject of nonabstinence goals for individuals is a matter of some controversy; a full review of the issue is not possible within the limitations of this book. Interested readers are referred to the section on controlled social drinking in Miller's *Behavioral Treatment of Alcoholism* [55] for a review of the current literature. *How to Control Your Drinking* [58] and *Drink to Your Health* [35] also present evidence favourable to the concept of controlled drinking treatment goals for individuals who drink excessively.

INDUSTRIAL ALCOHOLISM PROGRAMS

Only 3–5% of the alcoholic population is found on skid row. Where are the rest? It is estimated that more than 50% of the alcoholic population in North America consists of fully employed members of the labour force [59–61]. Facts about alcoholism in industry show that:

• One worker in 12 is an alcoholic.
• The cost to industry is very high. In Canada, an estimated $400 million is lost annually in wages and work related problems [62]. In the United States, an estimated $10 billion are lost annually due to work time alone.
• Alcoholic employees average 20 to 25 days absence a year because of excessive drinking, and in addition, have a greater number of absences for other illnesses [63]. They are sick two-and-one-half times more than normal employees [63].
• Alcoholics are fairly evenly distributed among occupations and industries, and are found at every level in a company—management through line worker, blue and white collar worker alike [64].
• The incidence of alcoholism is higher in employees with more seniority,

thus resulting in the loss of employees who are highly trained and valuable to the firm.

• The alcoholic employee is usually between 30 to 35 years and can conceal his alcoholism for 14 to 16 years after its onset. But his work performance deteriorates after four or five years [63].

• The alcoholic employee dies approximately 12 years earlier than his nonalcoholic counterpart.

For these reasons a growing concern with the identification and treatment of the employed alcoholic has resulted.

In the past, there has been a "stigma" associated with alcoholism, particularly in industry. An unwritten policy existed which stated "Thou shalt not drink, but if you do, both sides will cover for you until you become a full fledged alcoholic and then we will decide what to do with you." Both the employer and the employee have been reluctant to admit the existence of an alcohol problem, and only when the problem advanced to the later critical stages was it identified. By this time the recovery rate was low, rehabilitation time-consuming and costly, and impaired work performance high. Often the only choice conceivable to the employer was termination or retirement.

Occupational alcoholism programming began in the 1940s when a few large American companies decided to adopt more enlightened policies to deal with employees who had drinking problems. Alcoholics Anonymous was a strong influencing factor in the initiation of these early programs and still remains a vital force in the treatment of the alcoholic employee. These early programs used methods which were designed to identify only those employees with clearly marked signs of alcoholism. Consequently employees were identified only during the crucial later states.

Fortunately, industrial programs are now being designed which aim to successfully aid in the rehabilitation of the alcoholic employee. Employers and supervisors are being trained to identify alcohol-related problems early and prevent the further progression of the disease. By 1973, 621 industrial alcoholism programs were reported to be in at least some stage of development in the United States [59]. Also in existence were private and governmental organizations which offered their services in the development and implementation of new programs and acted as resource persons or consultants for any trouble spots the employer might encounter.

The most effective approach in the treatment of industrial alcoholism to date is the broadbrush approach [62] which focuses exclusively on monitoring job performance. Unacceptable performance is carefully documented and communicated by supervisors. It is their responsibility to identify and record all instances of absenteeism, lateness, mistakes on the job, inefficiencies, and other job performance problems. The supervisor does not attempt to diagnose or label the employee in any way. This approach eliminates the need for unqualified persons to confront "suspected" employees about their "drinking problems." Any confrontations that occur are related to a legitimate management concern—job performance. Only about half of the cases identified by Employee Assistance Programs are related to drug abuse. Other employee concerns are marital, financial, psychological, physiological, and vocational. Identifying and eliminating any problem causing poor work performance is cost reducing to the employer as well as beneficial to the employee.

A recent approach developed by the National Council on Alcoholism is the joint union-management approach, which seeks to co-operate with both union and management. It includes a joint policy statement between union and management, and the creation of management-union committees which make all the decisions regarding the operation of the program. Like the broadbrush approach, performance criteria are used for identifying employee problems. The only major difference between the two approaches is that the joint union-management approach deals only with alcohol-related problems and rejects the use of any term which does not clearly identify the program as an alcoholism program.

Industry is structured so that the work world provides an optimal setting for motivating the dependent person to seek treatment. Sometimes an employee considers his job and steady income as the most important element in his life and will allow everything around him—friends, family, home, and material possessions—go before letting his job go. It provides him with financial reinforcement, social approval, and self satisfaction.

The work setting is also ideal for identifying alcoholic problems. The employee's daily performance is visible and can be monitored. When confronted with facts of deteriorating work performance, the employee will more likely admit that his poor performance is caused by the use of alcohol, a fact which he has probably denied to himself and others.

Recovery is much more likely with employed persons than with unemployed or socially deprived or deteriorated people. Success rates as high as 85% have been claimed by some employers, but on the average better than two out of three recover, still a highly encouraging statistic [59, 62, 63].

ROLE OF THE SUPERVISOR

The supervisor plays a crucial role in identifying the alcoholic employee. He is often the first to recognize the problem and his co-operation is the key to the successful rehabilitation of the individual. Often supervisors are reluctant to take corrective action, especially when the employee has a long record of dependability—"He's the best man I've got, when he's here." However, supervisors should be made aware that the alcoholic employee runs an increased risk in the areas of physical and mental deterioration, marital breakdown, emotionally disturbed children, and suicide.

IDENTIFICATION OF THE ALCOHOLIC EMPLOYEE

The effectiveness of an industrial program is based on the supervisor's ability to identify and record all signs and symptoms related to poor work performance, whether directly related to alcoholism or not. The supervisor should be aware of these symptoms and alert for their appearance so that early recognition and early treatment may occur:

Poor Work Performance. Impaired performance, lowered productivity, carelessness, errors in judgment, laziness, sloppiness, covering up mistakes, early fatigue, and spasmodic performance.

Absenteeism. Increased frequency of days or half-days off work, absenteeism following paydays, or Monday and Friday afternoons.

Physical Appearance. Deterioration of appearance, sloppiness, lack of concern about hair and dress, or, conversely, a marked improvement in appearance.

Poor Health. Poor physical and mental well-being, increased medical claims, increased nervousness, swelling or flushing of the face, hand tremors, red or bleary eyes, nausea, hangovers, irritability, gastric upsets, or memory loss of recent events.

Safety. Frequent injuries, carelessness causing accidents, increased accidents off the job, and impaired driving charges.

Poor Work Relations. Friction with co-workers, lowered morale, bad executive decisions, sensitivity about drinking, or avoidance of boss or superiors.

INTERVIEWING PROCEDURES

Once poor work performance has been identified and documented, the first step a supervisor (or other designated person) must make is a corrective interview. Here are a few basic interviewing techniques (with minor author's revisions) prepared by M.D. Dalgliesh, Industrial Consultant, Alberta Alcoholism and Drug Abuse Commission.

1. Prepare a Written Fact Sheet. The first interview should be based on previously recorded facts relative to work performance, attendance, reliability, attitudes and habits, physical appearance, safety, and any other points related to reduced productivity.

2. Keep Discussion on the Subject. The employee may try to divert the discussion to irrelevant subjects. Be firm and keep the problem in perspective.

3. Offer Assistance. Impress him with a willingness to help him find a solution but firmness in pointing out that his actions have put his employment in jeopardy and that he is expected to correct the situation.

4. Be Optimistic. When a decision on appropriate action has been reached, approach every case as an assured success and make a sincere effort to achieve that success.

5. Avoid Meaningless Threats. All reasonable effort to bring the problem into the open may fail. When this happens, there is no alternative but to invoke the disciplinary action of company policy.

6. Never Cover Up. Personal friendship should never be used as an excuse to cover up an employee's problem. It can only delay proper corrective action and may rebound with bigger problems for everyone involved.

7. Do Not Diagnose. Avoid making any diagnosis or telling an employee he is misusing a drug. The interviewer's concern is with his job performance.

8. Do Not Betray Confidence. The confidentiality of the employee must be kept at all times. Information given is intimate and personal. At the same time, he must understand a responsibility to management. A pledge of confidence should never be made that cannot be kept.

9. Closing the Interview. The interview should close with mutual agreement on positive action. Do not prolong interviews when everything that needs to be said has been said by both parties.

REFERRAL PROCEDURE

If the employee admits to having a problem involving alcohol, the interviewing person should make the appropriate referral. Some companies have their own medical and counselling personnel, while most make referrals to outside sources. There are also many community-based organizations which are readily accessible. It is important to the recovery of the employee that he not be referred to a treatment facility that he find demeaning. He has already been faced with the ego-bruising admission that he has a drinking problem, and an inappropriate referral may threaten the motivation inspired by skillful company counselling. Elsewhere in this book, organizations involved in the treatment of the alcoholic have been described and these alternatives must be considered prior to referral. If the employee takes an outside referral, he is expected to improve his work performance during treatment. If after a reasonable period of time work performance remains unacceptable, the employee will be subject to disciplinary procedures.

If the employee denies a problem or refuses help, no further action is necessary at this time. He should clearly understand, however, that there must be an immediate improvement in his work performance. A definite appointment should be made for a further interview. If, at the second interview the employee's work performance has improved, he should be encouraged but must understand that·any relapse or deterioration in work performance will not be tolerated.

If, on the other hand, work performance has not improved, he should be confronted with the documented facts, and be told that something is obviously affecting his work. At this time he should be referred for a full medical examination. If the employee refuses to take the medical examination or if the medical examination confirms that alcohol misuse is the principal problem and the employee persists in refusing to accept help, there is no alternative but to invoke disciplinary action on the basis of company policy.

COMPANY POLICIES

One of the most crucial prerequisites to developing an alcohol program is the adoption of an explicit formal company policy. It should be known and understood by all members of the organization. The support and co-operation of management, union members, supervisory personnel and line workers alike is necessary for the program to be truly effective. Policies vary according to the particular needs of the organization and the specific type of approach. Here is a sample policy which has been suggested by the Addiction Research Foundation of Ontario.

A SUGGESTED EMPLOYER POLICY STATEMENT ON ALCOHOL AND OTHER DRUG ABUSE

1. The organization recognizes that alcohol and other drug abuse can lead to serious health and behaviour problems affecting many areas of a person's life.
2. For purposes of the policy, alcohol and other drug abuse which interfere with an employee's health and, in turn, his work performance, are defined as treatable illnesses.
3. The organization's concern with alcohol and other drug abuse is limited

strictly to their detrimental effects on the employee's health and, in turn, performance on the job.

4. The organization expects this policy will encourage employees to take early advantage of treatment on a voluntary basis.

5. However, based upon documented deteriorating job performance, as noted by the supervisor, a mandatory treatment referral will be arranged in conjunction with a company-designated physician. If the employee refuses the help that is offered and his job performance does not improve, the employee will be subject to the company's disciplinary procedure.

6. The confidential nature of the problem and various records will be preserved as this policy provides for application of regular sickness and health benefits.

7. Implementation of this policy will not result in other special regulations, privileges, or exemptions from the standard administrative practices applicable to job performance.

8. The organization assumes responsibility for the training of personnel regarding this problem.

JOB-BASED RISKS

Four major categories of factors related to work which enhance the risk of alcoholism have been identified as follows:

1. Lack of Visibility. Freedom to set work hours, positions which cause the employee to spend time away from the work setting, or absence of clear goals, with no work performance evaluation.

2. Absence of Structure. Work addiction, work-role removal, occupational obsolescence, or new work statuses.

3. Absence of Social Controls. Required on-the-job drinking, informal power struggles, or increased job mobility into a stressful position with no controls.

4. Miscellaneous Risk Factors. Severe role stress, competitive pressure, presence of illegal drug users on the premises, sheer boredom, or lack of a sense of personal fulfillment [65].

While the original "cause" of the deviance may be related to other factors outside the work world, these risk factors have been seen to reinforce and aggravate the drinking problem. Attention to eliminating as many of these risk factors from industry as possible may help to control some of the deviance that occurs within the work setting [65].

WORKING WOMEN AND THEIR DRINKING BEHAVIOUR

The incidence of alcoholism in women in general is on the rise. Women are gradually moving out of the home into the business and professional world where they are confronted with men's roles and obligations, which may cause anxiety, conflict and new temptations. Younger girls are starting to drink more and more and it has become more acceptable for a woman to drink. These young women may represent a large portion of the alcoholics of the future.

In spite of the rise of alcoholism in women, there has been insufficient research related to the female drinker [66–70]. Most psychiatric, psychological and sociological theory about alcoholism has focused on men [70]. Employee assistance programmes designed to identify "problem drinkers" consistently identify a much lower proportion of female drinkers than male drinkers. Treatment programmes now typically report a 3:1 ratio of men to women (Donwood Institute; Ottawa-Carleton Centre of Addiction Research Foundation of Ontario; Alcoholics Anonymous). Yet one Toronto treatment agency specializing in occupational referrals reports that it serves 20 men for every woman [71]. An Ontario industry reported 4 women referrals out of 80 for alcoholism treatment in 1976. This industry employs 37% women.

Why are employed women with drinking problems *not* being identified for treatment? One likely reason, previously mentioned, is the lack of research on female drinkers particularly those employed. How can the female "problem drinker" be identified when so little is known about her? Another possible reason is that many women are "closet drinkers," due to the heavy stigma still associated with women and alcohol use. Boyle and Pinder [71], in their excellent review of women, alcohol, and the workplace state that:

> It is in relation to women becoming alcoholic in the workplace that the issue of concealment takes on special meaning. It is possible that such women will make every effort to appear socially integrated. One study indicates that 80% of women diagnosed as alcoholic never missed work because of drinking and retained their jobs. Another study found that 20 of 25 employed women in the sample had never missed work (P. 32).

In the past fewer women were seen for treatment, and those who were seen were much sicker than men. Perhaps only those who are seriously ill or in great difficulty with abnormal environmental stresses exposed themselves. Many researchers suggest that employment has perhaps the most clearly positive effects on women's health of any variable investigated to date. Studies have been reported that show that working women have fewer symptoms, fewer disability days, and less anxiety than nonworking women.

Chambers (1975) reports the same findings. Perhaps working alcoholic women appear much healthier than their nonworking counterparts and are therefore less visible.

The Donwood Institute [72] reported that out of 798 alcoholic patients seen in 1975, 92% of the men and 48% of the women were in the labour force. Of those employed, 15% of the men had been referred by their employers while only 4% of the women had been referred by their employers. The sex difference here is certainly notable. What is it about the working woman alcoholic that she can conceal herself so well? Perhaps with further research on the alcoholic woman in the workplace the answers to these questions will become more evident.

Chapter 5

SPECIFIC TREATMENT INTERVENTIONS

IN THIS chapter we present some of the more important specific treatment interventions used by therapists from a variety of professional persuasions. Thus we are not implying that all of these would be applied to a given client or in a given general treatment program. However, all may be applicable and useful in an appropriate context.

ANTABUSE (DISULFIRAM)

Disulfiram is often used as an adjunct to psychotherapy. If taken regularly it serves as a deterrant to resumption of drinking by the patient who wants to abstain but is uncertain about his ability to do so. The drug owes its effectiveness to the fact that the ingestion of alcohol will, in interaction with antabuse, produce some very unpleasant reactions such as extreme nausea or vomiting. The sobriety associated with regular use of disulfiram enhances the person's ability to employ more traditional group or individual approaches. Disulfiram is often used for 3−12 months following detoxification.

A major problem with disulfiram treatment is that the patient may choose to take himself off medication and, after 48 hours, resume drinking. Lubetkin et al. [1] report that less than 1% of all patients continued to take antabuse after release from the hospital. Therefore, it is highly important that the taking of such medication be monitored by the patient's worker, spouse, probation officer, employer, or any other responsible party with a firm interest in the patient's sobriety. Research [2, 3] suggests that patients who are compulsive, older, socially stable, and motivated, and who likely have had blackouts do better on disulfiram. Those who are depressed and those with sociopathic traits do worse.

MINOR TRANQUILIZERS AND ANTIDEPRESSANTS

Research to date [4-6] suggests that such drug treatment of alcoholism is largely ineffective. Clinical experience suggests that the prescription of medication as an adjunct to psychotherapy is often counterproductive. The potential for abuse of drugs (antidepressants possibly excepted) by those who abuse alcohol is great. Clinicians with experience in the field of alcohol abuse avoid long-term treatment with minor tranquilizers and sedatives. Apart from the addiction potential of most drugs used in the treatment of alcoholism, their prescription reinforces the assumption of many patients that their solutions to life problems (such as anxiety, depression, sexual dysfunction, marital break-up, and vocational dissatisfaction) may be provided by chemical substances. Seasoned workers attempt to address, from a broad basis, the problems maintaining the patient's alcohol abuse and to inculcate alternate, nonchemical ways of coping with such problems. New coping skills provide positive alternative responses to excessive drinking behavior and provide the client with a new view of himself— namely that he can assume an active and responsible role in his own adjustment.

As a final point on this matter, it is useful to monitor the drug usage of alcoholic clients wherever possible (through urinalysis, blood sampling, or breath analysis), that is whether or not the patient has abused drugs prior to treatment. The alcoholic on disulfiram can still take excessive doses of barbiturates, tranquilizers, even heroin, and end up with two or more dependencies rather than one. In the event that the alcoholic patient is prescribed minor tranquilizers, supervised urine samples should be collected and analyzed to ascertain that drug usage is within prescribed amounts. The risk is that such patients will increase the frequency of administration and the amount of the dosage over time.

HALLUCINOGENS

LSD (lysergic acid diethylamide) enjoyed considerable interest about a decade ago; more recently, interest has waned and currently is not widespread. Initial research on LSD, while enthusiastic, was largely uncontrolled and anecdotal. Controlled studies [7-10], however, showed at at least transient short-term effects. Occasionally of course, those who take LSD may have negative experiences which do not help overcome the addiction and may even lead to a decrement in personal adjustment. Some researchers and clinicians nonetheless feel that the question remains open and that future investigations on LSD in different settings and in a different social and legal climate may demonstrate its effectiveness as an agent in the treatment of alcohol abuse. Moreover, it is unfortunate that the present social-legal climate has even discouraged the experimental use (by qualified workers) of a therapeutic agent which could be of help to those suffering from alcoholism.

BIOFEEDBACK

One of the most common problems faced by patients in treatment is their inability to achieve satisfactory levels of relaxation. Whether this disability predates or is a result of excessive drinking is unclear. Recent methods of training patients to achieve deep levels of relaxation involve biofeedback procedures [11]. Biofeedback procedures apply feedback technology to physiological systems. While these systems have traditionally been regarded as beyond voluntary control, biofeedback provides a means of bringing such functions into our consciousness thereby allowing learning and control to take place.

Relaxed states can be achieved by using electroencephalographic devices to monitor and display alpha brain waves, electromyographic feedback to reduce muscle tension, or galvanic skin response feedback. Auditory or visual signals provide the client with immediate data regarding the state of his body or brain waves. While anecdotal reports exist as to the impact of biofeedback procedures on drinking behavior, controlled studies with results are only now becoming available. A study by Steffen [12], for example, found that electromyographically induced relaxation (reduced muscle tension) resulted in reduced drinking, as well as lower muscle tension levels, and less subjective anxiety.

GROUP THERAPY

Unlike the above techniques which rely on medication or sophisticated technology, group therapy represents the first method of treating alcoholism described in this section, which hinges on the client *relating to another person or persons in a therapeutic setting.* Although group therapy is virtually required by custom in many inpatient and outpatient programs, the evaluation of its utility in the treatment of alcoholics by researchers in the field is mixed. Forrest [13] states that "group treatment approaches are presently perhaps the most promising treatment model specific to the problem of alcoholism. This opinion has a strong clinical experience basis, as well as research basis" (p. 93). Numerous other practitioners [14—16] enthusiastically regard group psychotherapy as the treatment of choice for alcohol dependent individuals. Baekeland et al. [17] however, in a review of alcohol treatment research argue that "the evidence in favor of (group therapy) is extremely marginal" and call for "well designed controlled studies" (p. 265).

A number of studies do cast doubt on group therapy's effectiveness with alcoholics. Westfield [18] reports on a group of 123 inpatients who completed a treatment program consisting of group therapy, Alcoholics Anonymous, work therapy, and recreational programs. Of the 60 who completed the program, 29 were abstinent or improved at the end of each year, an overall "success" rate of 24%. Using abstinence at one year as the criterion for improvement, Pokorny et al. [19] reported that only 25% of their group therapy patients were treatment successes. Wolff [20] reported a six month abstinence rate of 14.6% for his group therapy participants. Further doubt

on the effectiveness of group therapy for alcoholics is cast by Kish and
Hermann's [21] finding that 16 hours of group therapy had "no significant
effect on improvement rates" (p. 634), and that their 22% improvement
rate at one year was not significantly bettered by other treatment programs
with 64 hours [22] and 120 hours [23] of group therapy respectively.

Feher [24] has addressed the problems involved in group psychotherapy
with alcoholics particularly in the early stages of the treatment process. He
outlines three primary stumbling blocks that group therapists face in
conducting such groups:

1. Alcoholics' resistance to dealing with the task at hand, namely, their
dependency on alcohol;
2. Their tendency to define each other solely as "alcoholics" rather than
individuals who, while dependent on alcohol, may also be "defined" as
husbands, wives, office workers, carpenters, lawyers, students, or grand-
mothers. If healthier modes of living are to be assimilated, it is important
for group members to be able to operate from a wider frame of reference
and to see each other having a variety of social roles. It is not unheard of
for alcoholics who have abstained for many years, to abuse alcohol as a
way of maintaining the security and comraderie of alcoholic support
groups. That such self-definition can be destructive at times is clear; and
3. The variability with which alcoholic patients progress in group
therapy, the diversity in levels of intellectual, social, and psychological
functioning, and the consequent differences in patient ability to serve as
constructive change agents for each other.

Many inpatient and outpatient treatment programs utilize groups as the
primary therapeutic modality. Groups occupy considerable professional
time and absorb a substantial portion of the budgets of many treatment
programs. To assure maximum value for treatment dollars spent in such
programs, every effort must be made to determine the effectiveness of the
treatment techniques used. However, the authors of this manual would
suggest that the group therapies be evaluated within the inpatient or
outpatient programs themselves, since a great variety of therapy techniques
may be applied by different group leaders. For further reading on the
major group therapy orientations, the reader is referred to volumes by
Shaffer and Galinsky [25] and Lieberman, Yalom and Miles [26].

The following are some specific treatment interventions which could be
employed in group or individual (one-to-one) therapy.

CLIENT-CENTRED (ROGERIAN) THERAPY

This approach's emphasis on worker demonstration of empathy, positive
regard, and warmth for the client is important throughout the treatment

process, and critical in the early development of the worker-client relationship. Carl R. Rogers has been the primary exponent of the client-centred approach to therapy. Modifications in his views over the past 35 years of Rogers' research, clinical practice and writings are clear in his major publications [27−29].

RATIONAL-EMOTIVE THERAPY

Many alcoholic individuals possess irrational self-defeating ideas which contribute to their leading anxiety-laden, unhappy, and frequently hostile lives. Albert Ellis, a New York psychologist, developed a system of psychotherapy designed to modify the "self-talk" of his clients who tended to be perfectionistic, self-damning, and other-directed. Research by rational-emotive adherents suggests that modification of client belief systems significantly improves client behavior.

The rational-emotive therapist seeks to minimize the client's self-defeating ideas and to replace them with more realistic ways of viewing life. The therapist moves toward the latter goal by listening carefully for the "shoulds," "musts," or "oughts," and quickly pinning down the few basic irrational ideas motivating the client's disturbed behavior. The irrational ideas, not the client, are attacked and invalidated and he is shown how to replace such self-defeating ideas with rational, empirically-based ideas. Awareness of client irrational ideas is an important component of each worker's treatment efforts. Ellis' rational-emotive approach to therapy is described in a series of publications over the past two decades [30−33].

REALITY THERAPY

Reality therapy is a common sense approach to behavior change which stresses the "here and now" problems of the client, and the client's responsibility for making desired positive change. Developed by William Glasser, a psychiatrist, in the 1950s, reality therapy offers a means of addressing the alcoholic's tendency to project blame, to evade personal responsibility, to focus on historical events rather than the present, and to make excuses for not following up on treatment-related plans. It is essentially a no-nonsense approach which insists that the client accept responsibility for his behavior and that the client not use past events as excuses for behaving irresponsibly in the present. Reality therapy shares behavior therapy's interest in present behavior. It is not insight oriented nor does it seek to produce behavior change through exploration of client feeling. Plans for change are important in reality therapy and the reality therapist devotes time to "pinning down" client plans, for example, to search for employment, modify his relationships with others, or other specific real goals. Commitments to carry out such plans are required of the client and no excuses for failure to follow plans are accepted. Clients are confronted with their failures and of their responsibility for any resultant unpleasant consequences, but the therapist does not impose punishment. New plans or modifications of the untried or unsuccessful old plans are developed and the client is assisted to make a commitment to follow through with his plan. Descriptions of reality therapy may be found in Glasser's *Reality Therapy* [34] and *Positive Addiction* [35].

TRANSACTIONAL ANALYSIS

Transactional Analysis (TA) is a theory of personality organization developed by Eric Berne, a psychiatrist, in the mid 1950s. Although TA's concepts and techniques are centred in the group situation, it is not uncommon for its ideas to be applied in psychotherapy with individuals. Berne postulated that every individual possesses three ego states, namely, the Parent (replay of parental and other authority figures, arbitrary, nonperceptive, noncognitive), the Adult (rational, data processing, prediction making, non-affective) and the Child (feeling, thinking, and behaving as a child, probably under age seven; source of spontaneity and joy). TA also postulates that individuals follow life "scripts" fashioned early in life; such scripts may include "con-man," "alcoholic," or "failure" on the one hand, or the more positive "biologist," "good-guy," or "success" on the other. "Games" are postulated to advance the person's script. Steiner [16] describes three significantly different alcoholic games:

1. Drunk and Proud—The prototype is the junior executive or salesman who plays the game for the purpose of guilt-free expression of aggression through gambling, extra-marital relations, or some other socially adverse act.
2. Lush—This is most often played by depressed middle-aged, middle-income housewives or overburdened white-collar workers who are deprived of "strokes" (rewards), in particular in the context of sexual or emotional relations.
3. Wino—Wino is part of a self-destructive life script played by the skid row alcoholic who places his body on the line to force others to take care of him, at least temporarily.

Clearly written contracts are an integral part of TA. Each TA contract is written to meet the four basic requirements of legal contracts—mutual consent, valid consideration (definition of benefits conferred by the therapist and the client, definition of goals, criteria of goal achievement), competency (client is adult or minor with parental obligations to the contract, nonpsychotic, nonretarded, sober) and lawful object (contract is not in violation of any law or contrary to public policy or morals). Contracts are a reflection of TA's view that therapist and client share equal political power in the therapeutic relationship.

Claude Steiner's popular *Games Alcoholics Play* [16] describes TA's approach to the treatment of alcoholism. The reader is also directed to the primary works on TA by Berne [36, 37] and by Harris [38].

BEHAVIOR THERAPY

Behavior therapy is defined as "any of a large number of specific techniques that employ psychological (especially learning) principles to deal with maladaptive human behavior" [39, p. 1]. Behavioral techniques may include relaxation training, systematic desensitization, assertive training, operant conditioning and contingency contracting, as well as aversive conditioning and a variety of less commonly used techniques. Here we cover only the most widely used behavioral approaches, focusing on those most suited to the modification of alcohol abuse.

Historically, behavior therapy has its roots in the turn of the century behavioral experiments by Pavlov in classical conditioning and Thorndike in reward conditioning (a forerunner of modern operant conditioning). Until the 1950s, behavioral psychology remained essentially an academic laboratory discipline, with only rare application to the problems of human behavior. Following the publication of B.F. Skinner's *Science and Human Behavior* [40] and Wolpe's *Psychotherapy by Reciprocal Inhibition* [41], however, behavioral approaches began to assume an ever increasing importance to the mental health field. The 1960s and 1970s have witnessed the appearance of a large number of behavior therapy texts, behavior therapy journals, and a reorienting of many university departments of psychology, and to a lesser extent, psychiatry, to the behavioral model.

Behavior therapy owes much of its growth to its continued interest in experimental investigations of the effectiveness of its various techniques. Much of the current research in behavior therapy concerns the determination of which method is most effective with which problem. It may be that behavior therapy's greatest contribution is the importance that it attaches to approaching the field of psychotherapy from an empirical or observational basis.

Behaviorists consider behavior to be essentially a function of environment. Adaptive and maladaptive behavior alike are to a large degree, learned either directly through classical and operant conditioning or vicariously through modeling. Behaviorists value the tangible and the measureable. While some rigorous practitioners concern themselves only with observable behavior, a majority regard cognition (thinking) and affect (emotion) as being properly within the realm of modifiable behavior. Underlying "intrapsychic" causes are regarded by behaviorists as inaccessible, untestable and outside the scope of a scientific approach to human behavior. They contend that behavior can be manipulated without reference to any presumed underlying cause, and that such behavior change can be effected without resultant symptom substitution.

Behavior therapy differs from most therapeutic orientations in its utilization of behaviorally-defined treatment goals and the varied techniques which may be brought to bear on the problems to be treated. Behavior therapists, while not ignoring personal historical events, tend to be present oriented and interested above all in determining the factors maintaining the client's maladaptive behavior. Historical "insight" by itself is not often curative; even in those cases in which the client "understands" why he behaves the way he does, the behavior therapist seeks to systematically increase client adaptive behavior and decrease client maladaptive behavior. Many good books exist on the practice of behavior therapy [39, 42, 43] and the reader is encouraged to become familiar with their assumptions and techniques.

AVERSION THERAPY

The earliest behavioral technique applied to the treatment of alcoholism, aversion therapy, refers to the pairing of the sight, smell and taste of alcohol with a noxious stimulus. Aversive stimuli have included nausea induced by chemicals, faradic (electrical) shock to the arm or leg and nausea induced by verbal descriptions (covert sensitization). Electrical aversion conditioning was first used in the treatment of alcoholics nearly 50 years ago and served for many years as the primary behavioral intervention for alcoholism. However, Nathan [44] states that "we remain unconvinced that electrical aversion conditioning constitutes a definitive behavioral treatment for alcoholism" (p. 17).

Chemical aversion therapies appear to be somewhat more favourably regarded. Even so Baekeland, et al. [17], state that chemical aversion has not demonstrated "any special worth" and Nathan [44] suggests that while aversive conditioning with emetic drugs (which produce extensive vomiting) may be "somewhat more effective . . . its effectiveness in isolation from other concomitant behavioral and nonbehavioral treatments has not been established" (p. 38). Miller [45] adds that "these procedures are steadily losing popularity and most probably will be used minimally if at all in future behavioral alcoholism programs" (p. 175). Aside from effectiveness though, the loss of popularity for these methods is also undoubtedly due to a distaste on the part of many clinicians for inflicting pain upon another human being.

COVERT SENSITIZATION

Covert sensitization, a verbal aversion therapy, offers a promising alternative for the clinician to the above aversive conditioning techniques. Developed by Cautela [46, 47], covert sensitization utilizes the client's imagination to pair unpleasant, often nauseous, events with the (imagined) ordering of a drink, touching the glass to the lips, consumption of alcohol, etc.—all in the client's imagined natural environment. As such, the procedure is less expensive and less unpleasant than the other aversive techniques, can be employed by the client to enhance self-control in critical situations, and bears no medical contraindications. Furthermore, the therapist is able to reproduce the natural drinking environment, at least to the extent that the client is able to visualize it.

Covert sensitization consists of the following steps:

1. Client is taught deep relaxation;
2. When relaxed the client is told that drinking to excess is a strong learned habit which is very reinforcing and that the way to eliminate the drinking problem is to associate it with an unpleasant stimulus;
3. The client is asked while in a relaxed state to visualize an alcoholic drink and to signal with his right index finger when the scene is visualized;
4. He is next instructed to visualize that he is about to take the alcohol, then to imagine the full drinking sequence;
5. At the moment when the client brings the glass to his lips he is instructed to imagine an aversive stimulus, usually vomiting;
6. A relief scene is provided when the client turns away from the alcohol;
7. The worker provides instructions for the initial presentations; the client eventually is brought to self-instruct himself in the sequence and to practice twice a day on his own for homework;
8. Generally 20 presentations are made in the course of each covert sensitization session: ten scenes pair the intention of drinking with the aversive image. In ten alternating presentations the client has an urge to drink, feels some discomfort, decides not to drink, and immediately feels better;
9. The client is instructed to use the procedure whenever he feels a strong urge to drink; and
10. Additional scenes are developed, with consumption of a variety of the client's favorite beverages, being aversively affected in the various settings in which the client has abused alcohol in the past.

Treatment employing covert sensitization should continue for at least six to twelve months, and for at least six sessions after the cessation of drinking. Covert sensitization should be combined with other behavioral procedures that reduce the anxiety component of drinking and facilitate alternative methods of coping.

The following scene described by Cautela [47] illustrates the vivid images used in covert sensitization:

> You are walking into a bar. You decide to have a glass of beer. You are now walking toward the bar. As you are approaching the bar you have a funny feeling in the pit of your stomach. Your stomach feels all queasy and nauseous. Some liquid comes up your throat and it is very sour. You try to swallow it back down, but as you do this, food particles start coming up your throat to your mouth. You are now reaching the bar and you order a beer. As the bartender is pouring the beer, puke comes into your mouth. ... As soon as your hand touches the glass, you can't hold it down any longer. You have to open your mouth and you puke. It goes all over your hand; all over the glass and the beer. You can see it floating around in the beer. Snot and mucous come out of your nose. Your shirt and pants are all full of vomit. The bartender has some on his shirt. You notice people looking at you. You get sick again and you vomit some more and more. You turn away from the beer and immediately you start to feel better. As you run out of the bar room you start to feel better and better. When you get out into clean fresh air you feel wonderful. You go home and clean yourself up (p. 87).

Positive instructions regarding the therapeutic outcome contribute to the effectiveness of covert sensitization as they do with other procedures. For maximum impact, clients should be instructed that the conditioning effects are powerful and that if they so much as taste alcohol they will feel nauseous and vomit. Clinical studies and controlled research [45] indicate that covert sensitization offers the workers a viable means of decreasing the positive value of excessive drinking.

HYPNOSIS

Hypnosis is another verbal technique which may employ aversive imagery to effect reduced drinking or abstinence in its clients. Hypnosis has been used for a long time but has been the subject of only a few well designed experiments. Smith-Morehouse [48] reported a 53% improvement rate six months to two years post-treatment with a 37% improvement rate for his controls. The experimental clients in this study, however, volunteered for treatment by hypnosis. In a controlled study on the effects of hypnosis Edwards [49] found no significant gains in the direction of abstinence 12 months after treatment. Self-hypnosis is described in Rosenfeld's *The Book of Highs* [50]; the worker is also referred to Barber's *Hypnosis: A Scientific Approach* [51].

PROGRESSIVE RELAXATION TRAINING

Stress is probably the most often cited cause of excessive drinking. It has been assumed that alcohol reduces tension levels and that people drink in order to obtain release from tension. Research, however, on this tension-reduction hypothesis does not support the basing of treatment solely on stress reduction methods [52, 52]. Indeed, current evidence suggests that while a few drinks may reduce tension, a larger number of drinks may produce increased anxiety and depression. However, stress has been cited as being an important factor in the relapse of abstinent alcoholics. Such relapses may have been averted had the clients been familiar with and made use of alternate ways of coping with stress. One well-known, easy-to-learn means of reducing felt stress is progressive relaxation training.

Progressive relaxation techniques were first described 40 years ago by Jacobsen [54] as a means of facilitating muscle relaxation. They were subsequently adapted by Wolpe [41, 43] to generate the relaxed states required for his systematic desensitization procedure. The underlying assumption of relaxation training is that muscle tension and psychological tension are positively correlated and that, therefore, muscle relaxation and anxiety are incompatible states. Jacobson's progressive relaxation techniques involve the successive tensing and relaxing of voluntary muscles in an orderly sequence until all of the main muscle groups of the body are relaxed.

Relaxation exercises should not be hurried. The tension phase of the exercise should be from 5−10 seconds and the relaxation phase from 10−15 seconds. Be sure, moreover, that clients tense only one set of muscles at a time. Inadvertent tensing of additional muscle groups interferes with effective relaxation induction. Clients should be instructed to practice on their own each day to facilitate ready attainment of relaxed states. Some clients will require the assistance of a cassette tape recording of the procedure initially, but, after a few weeks, they should be encouraged to phase out the tape recorder once the procedure has been learned. Clients should be instructed also to note which of their muscle groups seems to hold the most tension. Eventually clients are able to achieve relaxed states in a "rapid" manner by selectively concentrating on those muscle groups that become tense, by deep breathing and by self-verbalizations to be calm and serene.

After about two to three weeks clients may begin to attain relaxed states, not by tensing all the muscles, but by mentally urging themselves to "let go" and by repeating to themselves the anxiety control words "calm and serene, calm and serene." This step may be followed by trying to generalize client relaxation responses from the worker's office or the client's bedroom to other situations involving different places, times and activities. Starting with relatively slow activities like relaxing with eyes open, clients may move through a series of more complex and demanding activities to the point where they are able to remain relaxed in the most demanding activities. One possible sequence for generalization of the relaxation response could be riding a bus, watching television, conversation, walking, shopping, playing sports, and talking to an angry person. Strategically placed 3 × 5 index cards may also assist the client by posing the question, "Are you relaxed?" or by instructing him to "Relax each time the phone rings" or "Relax on the hour." Further readings on relaxation training include Bernstein and Borkovec's *Progressive Relaxation Training: A Manual for the Helping Professions* [55] and Walker's *Learn to Relax* [56].

MEDITATION

Various forms of meditation may also be used to foster relaxed states. A number of reports have shown a reduction of general anxiety following Yoga and Transcendental Meditation. These two approaches provide an element of the "mystical" and offer a positive alternative to the more routine relaxation exercises.

Herbert Benson [57] one of the earlier researchers of Transcendental Meditation, has since developed a noncultic technique to elicit what he calls the "Relaxation Response." He has found that so long as the basic components of meditation are used, any of the historical or newly derived techniques produce the same physiological results—regardless of the mental device (mantra, sound, phrase, or other stimulus) used. An adapted form of the process he suggests is as follows:

1. Sit quietly in a comfortable position;
2. Close your eyes;
3. Deeply relax all your muscles, beginning at your feet and progressing up to your face. Keep them relaxed;
4. Breathe through your nose. Become aware of your breathing. As you breathe IN, say the word, "ONE," silently to yourself. As you breathe OUT say the word "TWO" in the same way. For example, breathe IN "ONE," OUT "TWO," IN "ONE," OUT "TWO," etc. Breathe easily and naturally;
5. Continue for 10 to 20 minutes. You may open your eyes to check the time, but do not use an alarm. When you finish, sit quietly for several minutes, at first with your eyes closed and later with your eyes opened. Do not stand up for a few minutes;
6. Do not worry whether you are successful in achieving a deep level of relaxation. Maintain a passive attitude and permit relaxation to occur at its own pace. When distracting thoughts occur, try to ignore them by repeating "ONE" "TWO." With practice, the response should come with

little effort. Practice the technique once or twice each day. The digestive processes seem to interfere with the elicitation of the Relaxation Response; many individuals therefore practice the technique before breakfast and/or before dinner.

While a number of retrospective, uncontrolled reports [58] suggest that the practice of Transcendental Meditation (TM) leads to decreased alcohol intake, controlled experimental investigations of the impact of TM on alcoholic individuals remain to be conducted.

SYSTEMATIC DESENSITIZATION

Systematic desensitization (SD) consists of presenting anxiety producing situations arranged in a hierarchy to clients in states of relaxation induced by progressive relaxation training. In the same way that a parent may introduce his or her child to the ocean a step at a time, SD involves presenting to the client's imagination only those situations that produce little or no discomfort. As the client habituates to a given scene in the hierarchy and succeeds, more anxiety-producing situations are introduced.

SD is applicable to the elimination or reduction of fears instrumental to the client's abuse of alcohol but not directly to the use of alcohol itself. Clients who are skilled but anxious in social situations may be treated using SD, imaginally or *in vivo* (in the natural environment). The workman who drinks on the job to allay his fear of heights or the woman drinking to assuage inordinate fear of rejection by her spouse may likewise be treated using this procedure. Studies utilizing SD to this end [59-63] report favorable outcomes.

SD is most appropriate when the client has only a *few* specific fears, is able to achieve relaxed states and to visual scenes which cause anxiety. Fortunately, the majority of clients with fears meet these criteria. The components of SD include:

1. *Relaxation training*—"Progressive Relaxation Training".
2. *Visualization of scenes causing anxiety*—Clients typically have little trouble creating vivid mental pictures of events just witnessed but occasionally will complain of difficulty remembering those occurring in the past. The following procedure is used to enhance the client's visual imagery.

The client is given homework tasks to periodically examine an object, then close his eyes and try to imagine what he has just seen. At first the client should visualize familiar objects in his home and immediately imagine the object. Later the client can be instructed to visualize less familiar objects and allow longer and longer amounts of time between looking at the object and creating the image. Finally, events can be imagined which are anxiety producing. In this regard it is usually best to start *first* with events that elicit *little* anxiety. Imagining events which elicit anxiety should be conducted in the therapist's office, since presentation of images which produce high levels of anxiety may require immediate intervention.

With the help of the worker the client determines usually 10—20 orderly steps in a *hierarchy* relevant to the feared object or situation. The first step would be the least anxiety-producing. For example the claustrophobic might be asked to first imagine, while relaxed, being in a large open area alone. His final scene may involve standing in a crowded elevator for 15 minutes.

3. *Subjective Units of Disturbance (SUD)*—Generation of scenes and assessment of their anxiety potential is frequently aided by the use of SUD reading on their anxiety level. Readings range over a 100 point scale, zero being completely anxiety-free and 100 being maximally anxious. Systematic desensitization is enhanced when the scenes in the hierarchy are no more than five SUD units apart.

The above components are then brought together in the following therapeutic procedure:

1. Generate relaxed state;
2. Present scene from desensitization hierarchy (beginning with least anxiety-arousing scene). The client signals with his finger when the scene is visualized and continues to imagine the scene for five to seven seconds;
3. After five to seven seconds of scene presentation instruct client to "erase" the scene and to return to deep relaxation. Inter-scene relaxation is facilitated by deep breathing, by instructions to relax and to be "calm and serene," and by visualizing a pleasant scene, (lying comfortably on a warm beach, resting on top of a water bed, or conjuring up some other pleasing scene). Request the SUD level generated by the scene presented and make note of it for future presentations.
4. Repeat scene and continue in order to *next* scene in hierarchy if no anxiety is generated in two successive presentations of 20 seconds each.
5. If anxiety is generated by the scene, the client signals the therapist, terminates the scene and continues relaxing for about 30 seconds. It may take three to seven presentations of each scene or more before its presentation produces no anxiety.

When the client can *imagine* all scenes in the hierarchy without anxiety he is instructed to engage in the hierarchical scenes in the *real* world. (Indeed, it is preferable to carry out the desensitization procedure *in vivo* when possible. Contraindications for *in vivo* desensitization may be excessive anxiety or unavailability of feared objects or situations.)

The *in vivo* procedure is similar—the client exposes himself to the fear stimulus in a relaxed state. If he experiences anxiety he pauses, relaxes and thinks through the elements in fantasy until he is sufficiently poised to proceed *in vivo*. As he masters each scene he proceeds to the next in the hierarchy. The client is encouraged to use this same procedure whenever he encounters situations that cause him to feel anxious. He is taught to control his anxiety through "anxiety control cues." For most clients this involves taking a deep breath, holding it, and breathing out quietly. The "anxiety control cue" breaks up the autonomic processes associated with anxiety and it becomes a conditioned stimulus for relaxation.

COGNITIVE MODIFICATION

Clients who are anxious in many interpersonal situations are probably better served by cognitive modification than by systematic desensitization. Cognitive modification [64, 65] blends the relaxation training and hierarchies of systematic desenitization with the ideas of Albert Ellis [30–33] on client self-verbalization. The primary difference is that the client in cognitive modification confronts the anxiety-producing scene and endeavors to cope with it through appropriate healthy self-verbalizations incompatible with previous irrational ideas ("I must be the best on my job") and by self-instructions to relax and to breathe deeply.

Experimental studies so far have been primarily limited to treatment of test and speech anxiety; studies pertaining to modification of alcoholics' self-verbalizations remain to be conducted. For further reading the worker is referred to Ellis [30–33] and Lazarus and Fay [66].

THOUGHT STOPPING

Thought stopping (Wolpe) is an effective and simple procedure for reducing and eliminating self-defeating trains of thought. In the treatment of alcoholics such thoughts would generally include urges to drink. Thought stopping is taught to the client in the following manner:

1. Ask the client to close his eyes and to describe out loud his urge to drink. He should increase the obsession to maximum intensity, then signal by raising a finger. When you note the raised finger, slap the table with your hand and yell, "STOP." Generally the client is startled and forgets about drinking for a minute. Tell the client that he can stop urges to drink by himself in the same way.

2. Same as above, except the client keeps his thoughts subvocal and signals when he begins to obsess. The therapist shouts "STOP!" when the client signals.

3. Client verbalizes the thought subvocally and shouts "STOP" aloud when he begins to obsess.

4. Same as above, except the client says "STOP" to himself *subvocally*. The client then practices this procedure several times and is given the following assignment:

"Carry a 3 × 5 card and pencil on your person at all times. Whenever you become aware that you are experiencing an urge to drink take the data card from your pocket and mark an "X" under the day's date. Then thought-block. Tense your body and yell subvocally at the urge to "GET OUT OF HERE." Attend to the external environment. Your attention is really up in *your head* when you obsess. Direct it to the world outside your body as though it were the first time you had ever seen it."

For a few clients thought stopping does not decelerate the urges to drink. Suggest substituting the self-administration of an aversive stimulus for the subvocal command to "STOP THE THOUGHT." In many cases the simple application of a rubber-band snap around the wrist is sufficiently disruptive and aversive to decelerate the alcohol urges. The client should not only self-punish, but record the frequency of the behaviors he punishes, yielding data on which to judge the efficacy of this procedure.

No studies are known to have investigated the efficacy of verbal or self-administered aversive thought stopping procedures on the frequency of client urges to consume alcohol.

POSITIVE SELF-CONCEPT ENHANCEMENT

Positive self-concept is a function of the relative frequency of positive and negative verbalizations *about* oneself *to* oneself. Thought stopping has been described as a means of decreasing negative self-defeating thoughts. Such a decrease, if accompanied by procedures to increase the frequency of positive self-verbalizations, could increase the feeling of client self-esteem.

Though positive self-thoughts are desirable to most people they don't always come easily. Clients can increase the frequency of positive self-thoughts by placing index cards with positive statements in strategic places around the house and in the car. Notes with positive statements can be fixed to cigarette packs, to make-up kits or to any personal belonging that is frequently viewed.

ASSERTIVE TRAINING

Assertive behavior refers to the ability to appropriately express personal rights and feelings in the presence of others. It advocates sensitivity on the part of the client to his own needs and feelings as well as the needs and feelings of others. The components of assertive behavior include nonverbal behavior, (eye contact, proper body posture and facial expressions, well-modulated speaking pattern) and verbal behavior (expression of positive and negative feelings, making requests, refusing unreasonable requests, asking why, talking about oneself, giving and taking compliments, giving and taking criticism, expression of anger, coping with others' anger and maintaining social conversations).

Assertiveness is not the same as aggressiveness as some clients may suppose and the differences should be clearly defined. Aggressive individuals tend to be concerned with only their own needs and feelings and are inconsiderate and unpleasant to be with. Assertive individuals, on the other hand, exercise their own rights *without* denying the rights and feelings of others. Another point to be made is that "assertiveness" is not a generalized trait equally evident regardless of social context. Quite the opposite, individuals tend to vary in their performance of the components of assertive behavior described above and tend furthermore to be effected by the interpersonal situation (for example, the woman who can refuse the door-to-door salesman's requests but not her mother's).

Assertive training is of particular relevance to the treatment of alcoholics. Marlatt [67] found that the three most common reasons for relapse in 48 abstinent clients were frustration and inability to express anger, inability to cope with social pressures to drink, and inability to resist strongly felt urges to drink. The first two reasons fall clearly within the province of assertive training. Experimental research [68–70] demonstrates that alcoholics increase their consumption of alcohol following interpersonal stress situations, whereas social drinkers are significantly more assertive and tend to actually decrease their use of alcohol following such situations. This suggests that the individual who abuses alcohol responds to interpersonal stress by drinking excessively rather than by being appropriately assertive. Other findings are that alcoholics perceive themselves as being much more assertive than they really are, have more difficulty with negative expressions than positive and consume more alcohol the less assertive they are. The evidence then suggests that client unassertiveness is related to excessive consumption of alcohol.

In the past five years several investigations [59, 71–73] have reported including assertive training in their treatment programs for alcoholics. In one such program [59] 11 out of 15 clients treated with assertive training and contingency contracting attained their goals while another two were significantly improved. In another study [73] increased assertiveness on the part of an alcoholic husband resulted in reduced consumption of alcohol and positive gains in the marital relationship.

Although diagnosis that a client is unassertive is relatively simple, the actual determination of the components of the unassertiveness and their situational variants may be more difficult. In assessment it is also important to determine whether the client is unassertive because he is immobilized by anxiety (in which case systematic desensitizaton may be indicated) or because he simply does not know how to be assertive (in which case assertive training is indicated). Self-report inventories such as the Rathus Assertiveness Schedule [74], the Lazarus Assertive Questionnaire [42], and the Assertiveness Inventory [75] help pinpoint specific areas of unassertiveness. Additional information can also be gathered by means of autobiographies outlining critical events in which the client behaved unassertively.

Although other procedures do exist, the most common technique for inculcating assertive behavior is behavior rehearsal, also known as role-playing. The advantage of behavior rehearsal is that it allows the client to practice new responses in a safe nonpunitive environment. The systematic training of assertive behavior using behavior rehearsal is as follows:

In the Office

1. The client enacts the behavior as he normally would.

2. The worker provides feedback, stressing the *positive* features, and pointing out shortcomings in an *accepting nonpunitive* fashion.

3. The worker assumes the client's role and models more desirable behavior. The client may assume the other person's role when appropriate.

4. The client enacts the behavior a second time, incorporating behavior changes suggested by worker feedback and modeling.

5. The therapist bountifully rewards improvement. If necessary, Steps 3 and 4 are repeated until both worker and client are satisfied with the response, and the client can engage in the response with little or no anxiety.

6. As for the expression of *negative* feelings, the client should be instructed to begin with a *relatively mild* response. Stronger responses may also be given in case the initial expression proves ineffective.

7. In expressing negative feelings, the client is urged to "own" his feelings and to direct his comments to the other person's behavior not the person himself. For example "I get so angry when you are late" rather than "you are an inconsiderate idiot!"

Out of the Office

8. The client is now ready to test his new assertiveness in the real world. Up to this point the preparation has taken place in a relatively secure environment. Once the client is comfortable and skilled in handling the target situation, however, he should be encouraged to proceed *in vivo.*

9. The client should also be encouraged to return as soon as practical following the *in vivo* trial, in order to review the effort. The worker should reward whatever degrees of success the person experiences, and offer continued assistance. It is also good to have the client keep a record of

how it goes, what he says, his feelings and so on in an assertiveness journal.

It is very important that the client's initial attempts at being assertive be chosen for their high potential of success, so as to provide reinforcement. A strong failure experience early in assertive training may well precipitate the premature termination of the client. Working through a hierarchy of interpersonal situations from least to most anxiety producing provides structure and helps assure that a client will not become involved in situations that he is not ready for.

One of the more common problems faced by problem drinkers attempting to abstain from or control their use of alcohol is drink refusal. Many simply can't say no to anything whether it be someone wanting money, just "a small favor," or an offer of "just one more drink." Many clients initially have difficulty refusing drinks but eventually, through worker feedback and modeling, develop considerable proficiency at it. The example below portrays a controlled drinker's post-treatment refusal of "just one more."

Friend: Come on, George, have one on me.
George: No thanks, I've had my limit for today.
Friend: Hey, one won't hurt you!
George: I'm sure you're right but I've had my limit for today.
Friend: Boy, you sound awfully unsociable!
George: I'm sure I do but I've had my limit and I'm not having any more tonight. Tell you what though, I'll have one of those Cokes there.

That this way of coping with offers of alcohol is more desirable than either taking the drink or getting angry and shouting obscenities seems obvious.

In the past five years many excellent books on assertive behavior have become available. Of all of them, *Your Perfect Right* [75] is probably the best one to begin with. It provides the client with the language tools needed to communicate personal aspects of unassertive behavior. Thus, the client becomes familiar with terms like "situation non-assertiveness" and is made aware of the difference between being aggressive and being assertive. Manuel Smith's book *When I Say No I Feel Guilty* [76] provides the unassertive or aggressive client with powerful assertive verbal skills such as "fogging," "broken record," and "negative inquiry." Female clients may be directed to *The Assertive Woman* [77] by Phelps and Austin.

SOCIAL SKILLS TRAINING

Social skill involves the art of relating well to other human beings. Alcohol abuse has long been associated with skill deficit in these areas: in some cases, alcohol provides the necessary lubricant for social interaction; in others alcohol serves to ease the loneliness of social isolation [78].

The subject of how to relate to others is much too large to cover adequately in this context. Fortunately many excellent books exist which offer materials concerning the development of communication skills and social abilities. Gordon's *Parent Effectiveness Training* [79], for example, while directed at "parents" is an excellent source for all people who wish to develop their communication skills. Knox's *Marriage Happiness: A Behavioral Approach to Counselling* [80] offers an array of behavioral treatment methods for marital problems. Techniques for initiating, maintaining and ending conversations, for meeting people, and for dealing with conflict are presented in detail in Gambrill and Richey's *It's Up To You: Developing Assertive Social Skills* [81]. Langer and Dweck's *Personal Politics: The Psychology of Making It* [82] covers the relationship between self-concept and the manner in which individuals relate to others. Written from essentially a behavioral vantage point, the authors discuss the principle of positive reinforcement in human relationships, information gathering and dissemination, how to make requests and impression management. George Bach and his colleagues [83-85] have also described the nature of intimate relationships and how to manage conflict and aggression within them.

CONTINGENCY CONTRACTING

Contingency or behavioral contracting is a form of operant conditioning which systematically defines desired behavior change and schedules rewards for observance and penalties for violation of the various contractual clauses. Other operant strategies such as token economy systems, contingency management, and manipulation of schedules of reinforcement have been applied effectively with alcoholic inpatients [45].

Operant procedures, and contingency contracting in particular, appear to have been applied less frequently in the treatment of outpatient alcoholics. Several studies [86-88] have demonstrated the impact of peer and spouse attention, monetary contingencies, and social and community reinforcement on alcohol use. An analogue study [89] showed that written contracts with alcoholic inpatients modified their use of alcohol and that the active component of the contracts was the reinforcement contingencies (points gained for drinking at or below the goal level, points lost for exceeding the goal level, points exchangeable for money). Instructions without contingencies were found to have little effect on alcohol consumption. Moreover, signed written agreements without contingencies had only a minor impact on drinking level.

Written contingency contracts have been used in the treatment of outpatient marital problems [90], and drug abuse [91, 92]. Miller [45] reports on the results of contingency contracting between a problem drinker and his wife. For excessive drinking the husband was required to pay $20.00 to his wife who was to spend it frivolously. His wife was also to withdraw her attention if he consumed over three drinks per day. The wife was required to pay a similar fine for negative statements regarding her husband's drinking. Both husband and wife provided increased attention and affection to each other for observing the requirements of the contract. The husband's problem drinking was brought under control within 30 days and was maintained at low levels at a six month follow-up. The one thing that all of these studies make clear is the need for clear specifications of individualized reinforcers. "One man's meat is another man's poison" is a saying that holds true for the determination of effective rewards and penalties in contingency contracts. Cautela and Kastenbaum's *Reinforcement Survey Schedule* [93] often proves helpful in determining effective reinforcers.

Effective contingency contracts for controlled drinking incorporate the concept of *stimulus control*. Stimulus control involves carefully analyzing the antecedents to excessive drinking and rearranging environmental cues to render excessive drinking a more difficult behavior to engage in. Such self-control maneuvers may include keeping liquor supplies low, drinking only at certain times of the day in certain places, drinking only with moderate drinkers, not drinking when fatigued, angry or anxious, drinking within specified limits (such as two 12-ounce bottles of beer per day), not re-ordering within 30 minutes, and alternating nonalcoholic beverages with alcohol beverages. Other conditions specific to the individual may be determined by examining the chain of events leading up to bouts of excessive drinking.

Effective contingency contracts will encourage client self-monitoring of alcohol consumption. It is well known that self-monitoring procedures have a moderating effect on the target behavior, particularly if the recording precedes the target behavior [94]. Furthermore, self-monitoring of alcohol use provides a more firm data base for determining the impact of the treatment approach adopted. Keeping a diary or log of events critical to the client's use or abuse of alcohol may also enhance treatment impact [95]. In sum then contingency contracts will likely be most effective when they:

1. Encourage client self-monitoring;
2. Identify antecedents to excessive drinking and describe alternate behaviors to engage in which are incompatible with excessive drinking; and
3. Define desirable behavior and the rewards for compliance and the penalties for contract violations.

Good contract writing takes practice, experience, and above all, a thorough understanding of each client. The following steps are involved in negotiating a contract with a client:

1. State the target behavior in specific and positive terms, in a way that it can be monitored numerically by frequency or length of time; state the conditions under which the behavior shall occur;
2. Determine the means of monitoring the target behavior;
3. Determine criteria for contractual compliance and violation;
4. Describe a variety of individualized consequences for compliance with or violation of the contractual clauses;
5. Apply rewards or penalties immediately upon contractual compliance or violation; avoid "burning-out" rewards or penalties by over-application—draw from a variety of rewards or penalties;
6. Throughout the contract be as specific as possible. Leave nothing to chance; make the contract as tight and as comprehensive as possible. Lengthy initial contracts always become shorter through amendment as the client becomes increasingly involved in self-management;
7. Be sure to sign the contract and have it witnessed. Copies of the contract should be made available to all signing parties;
8. As treatment proceeds, place more and more of the contractual management in the hands of the client. Reinforcement from the worker for contractual compliance or violation may be necessary initially. Eventually, however, such control should be shifted to the client who will reward and/or punish his own behavior. Self-reinforcement has been demonstrated to prolong the maintenance of self-control over time [96].

ADDITIONAL THERAPEUTIC APPROACHES

The treatment of alcohol abuse may also take into consideration the following additional approaches:

Educational and vocational counseling

This treatment should be coordinated through local community agencies and educational institutions.

Job placement

The therapist should work through government supported and/or private employment agencies.

Marital counseling

For a behavioral approach to marital discord refer to Knox's *Marriage Happiness* [80] and an article by Stuart [90].

Sexual dysfunction

For a behavioral approach to the treatment of sexual problems see the volumes by Jack S. Annon [97, 98].

Problems with children

See Gordon's well-known *Parent Effectiveness Training* [79] and McIntire's *Child Psychology: A Behavioral Approach to Everyday Problems* [99].

Obesity

For a behavioral approach to the treatment of obesity see Stuart and Davis' *Slim Chance in a Fat World* [100].

Physical exercises

Physical exercise has generally been overlooked as a factor in the treatment of problem drinkers. Yet a regular exercise program may serve as a potent response which is incompatible with excessive drinking. Such a concept is in accord with Glasser's idea [35] of positive addictions (jogging, meditation) and has some support from Gary and Guthrie's findings [101], that jogging one mile per day for 20 days improved their clients' cardiovascular functioning, self-esteem and sleeping patterns. Exercise also is a viable means of tension reduction. Excellent physical training prosXms are outlined in McCamy and Presley's *Human Life Styling* [102].

Nutrition

Nutrition is also an area that workers frequently overlook in their efforts to treat their alcoholic clients. A complete exploration of the role nutrition may play in alcohol is outside of the province of this book. Nonetheless it is difficult to ignore the statement of a leading nutritionist, Dr. Roger Williams [103] that "no one who follows good nutritional practices will ever become an alcoholic." Recent research conducted by Register and his colleagues [104] found that laboratory rats fed marginal diets of "junk food" (doughnuts, hot dogs, spaghetti, cake, candy, and cookies) drank significantly more of a 10% alchohol solution than rats provided nutritionally adequate food. Furthermore, when the "alcoholic" rats were switched to adequate diets their consumption of the alcohol solution decreased. Cheraskin and Ringsdorf's chapter on nutrition and alcoholism in *Psychodietetics* [105] describes some interesting initial reports by nutritionists on the effect of nutritional therapy of alcoholism. Related readings on nutrition may be found in Chapter 5 of *Drink to Your Health* [106] and in *Human Life Styling* [102].

Recreational counseling

It is not uncommon for those who abuse alcohol to gradually abandon positive recreational activities. The attendant loss of enjoyment of these activities and the movement away from a social environment in which moderate but not excessive drinking is condoned, propels the alcoholic individual further into his or her abuse of alcohol. Recreational behaviors incompatible with excessive drinking need to be redeveloped. Clients can be instructed to construct a list of all activities that they formerly found enjoyable but have not engaged in since drinking heavily and a second list of activities they have observed others enjoying and would be interested in learning. Some clients have difficulty recalling reinforcing activities they have done or imagining what else they might like to do. In such cases the Pleasant Events Schedule [107,108] may prove helpful. The Pleasant Events Schedule consists of a checklist of 160 activities which the client may rate in terms of enjoyment and frequency engaged in. The advantage of this approach is that it names activities for the client and, while not exhaustive, it is comprehensive enough for the client. Cautela and Kastenbaum's Reinforcement Survey Schedule [93] also provides a checklist of potentially reinforcing recreational activities.

Non-alcohol ways of getting "high"

Over the last decade there has been considerable discussion about chemically-induced altered states of consciousness. Throughout history mankind has sought to transcend his ordinary consciousness through chemical, and nonchemical, means. Alcohol was one of the first chemical means developed to alter man's consciousness and continues to be the primary drug in modern society. Some clients are sensitive to this issue and want to know how, if they are to modify their use of alcohol, they are to get "high." Two excellent resource books for concerns of this kind are Rosenfeld's *The Book of Highs* [50] and Otto and Mann's *Ways of Growth* [109].

In a comprehensive program many of the above general considerations will be accompanied by specific techniques to decrease the frequency of excessive drinking, increase the frequency of alternative behaviors incompatible with excessive drinking and generate environmental supports for abstinence or controlled use of alcohol. Recent research [88, 110, 111] has demonstrated the effectiveness of intervention programs which comprehensively approach the alcohol abuser. Such programs do not rely on single treatment modalities nor do they concern themselves only with the client's abuse of alcohol.

Chapter 6

DAY-TO-DAY TREATMENT OF THE ALCOHOLIC

IN THIS chapter we provide some guidelines for day-to-day work with the alcoholic client. Of course these cannot be separated from the considerations of the previous two chapters. However, the focus here is more on monitoring of the client's problems and progress, motivating the client to continue in treatment and determining direction and goals.

ASSESSMENT

To successfully treat alcohol abuse, the worker needs to know what goes on before, during, and after client consumption of alcohol. The factors which contribute to abusive drinking are specific to the client and can be identified correctly only by careful analysis. The people you are with, the time and place you drink, amount and type of available alcohol, concurrent activites, and emotional states can all influence client (and nonclient) drinking. Such antecedents to client abuse of alcohol should be carefully determined and considered in any treatment program. The reinforcing qualities of abusive drinking also require careful definition. Reinforcers may derive from the social environment or from altered psychological states. Although the subject of current controversy [1], tension reduction has been regarded as an important reinforcer for excessive drinking and has served as the basis for such interventions as systematic desensitization and assertive training. Excessive drinking may also serve to sedate personal failure, grief, boredom, low self-esteem, or depression.

More positively alcohol contributes to a state of euphoria, feeling "high." Taste can be important, as can the comraderie and social reinforcement from peers who are also heavy drinkers. Other motivators may include seeing others reinforced for heavy drinking, disinhibition of socially unacceptable behavior, and, for the client, the empathic attention of personnel in social service and alcohol abuse treatment agencies. These reinforcers are only suggestions. It is expected that a detailed investigation of each client's drinking pattern will produce reinforcers specific to each client. The following questionnaires have been developed to assist in the assessment of alcohol abuse and the situational factors involved in its maintenance (Tables 6.1−6.5, used to illustrate the questionnaires, will be found at the end of this chapter):

Michigan Alcoholism Screening Test (MAST)

This test [2, 3] consists of twenty-five items which measure the impact of excessive drinking on the client's physical, social, vocational, and legal status as well as getting an overview of the client's drinking history and patterns of alcohol use.

The client's score may range from zero to 53 (or more in some cases). A score of three points or less is considered nonalcoholic, a score of four points is suggestive, and a score of five points or more is considered to show alcoholism with increasing problems as the score increases. Of course, as we have stated previously, identification of a person as "alcoholic" is not as important as identification of alcohol related problems. For greater detail on use of the MAST, the reader is directed to Table 6.1 and primary references [2, 3].

Client Personal History

Modeled on Lazarus' Life History Questionnaire [4], the inventory in Table 6.2 covers basic demographic data, educational history, vocational history, health history, relationships with family and friends, treatment history, judicial history, and motivation for treatment. It is designed to be completed by the client at home. Its value is in terms of the breadth of information provided concerning the client's life, parts of which will bear further scrutiny and discussion throughout the treatment process.

Behavioral Assessment of Alcohol Abuse (BAAA)

The BAAA (Table 6.3) is modeled on the Drinking Profile by Marlatt [5]; it complements the Client Personal History by exploring in detail the antecedents, concurrent activites, and consequences of excessive drinking. It is designed to be completed by the client in the clinic with the worker. Card sorts of beverage preferences, effects of drinking, and reasons for alcohol abuse are required. The list of beverages and reasons for alcohol abuse are found on the last two pages of the BAAA.

Continuous Data Questionnaire (CDQ)

This life space survey (Table 6.4) reflects the broad base from which an increasing number of therapists operate. Completed every three months by the client, performance in work, education, family and social relations, judicial involvement, personality and emotional development, sexual functioning, physical health and level of motivation may be evaluated from initial assessment, through treatment and into the twelve month follow-up phase. Thus the CDQ is particularly valuable for assessing attainment of treatment goals and progress through treatment.

In addition to the alcohol-related assessment devices, therapists have developed a variety of instruments to assess the disorders, (anxiety, depression, unassertiveness, marital problems) concurrent with alcohol abuse. The reader is referred to Shelton and Ackerman's Homework in Counselling and Psychotherapy [6] for a description of the most common assessment instruments.

Review of the above materials provides a basis for a written report of the personal history and the etiology and treatment of the client's alcohol abuse and other problems. An example of a summary assessment of a client presenting for treatment of alcohol abuse is shown in Table 6.5.

COLLECTION OF BASELINE DATA

Prior to treatment intervention it is often useful to collect precise data about the nature of the alcohol abuse and its situational variants. Such daily information may be gathered via three sources:

1. The client;
2. "Significant others": family, friends, employer; and
3. Random breath-alcohol tests in the natural environment.

Client self-report of drinking is of doubtful utility. It is subject to forgetfulness, distortion, and the social approval (or disapproval) of the client's worker. Instead of such global reports, the client may be instructed to keep behavioral information on index cards, specifying the following:

Date/Time: _____ Place: _____ with whom: _____
type: _____ amount:_____ concurrent activities:___

emotional state: _____

Client accounting of alcohol intake may be checked against the reports of the client's spouse, parents, friends, or work associates as the case may be. This information may also be inaccurate so it is advisable to collect reports from a number of persons having frequent and non-prejudiced contact with the client.

Clients are encouraged to expand on their index card data in personal log books or diaries. The client is asked to note the situations in which he drank excessively and is encouraged to describe the circumstances in as much detail as possible. Nonalcohol events such as marital or vocational dissatisfaction can also be noted and brought to therapy sessions to help formulate goals and monitor the effects of treatment intervention. For those whose writing skills are deficit, speaking into cassette recorders on a daily basis serves as an adequate subsitute for the written log.

The most useful means of assessing and monitoring client alcohol use involves the twice weekly random sampling of breath-alcohol levels of clients in the natural environment. A brief procedural manual is found in Table 6.6. Simple balloon-like devices such as the model SM6 MOBAT produced by Lucky Laboratories [7] or newer solid state machines such as the ALERT model J2A 1000 produced by Borg Warner offer portable means of obtaining adequate accurate estimates of client blood alcohol concentrations. Contractual rewards and penalties for the outpatient client may be made contingent on monitoring outcome. Needless to say, such *in vivo* monitoring is of the greatest importance whether the object is collection of baseline data, evaluation of treatment effects or maintenance of gains following the completion of treatment.

MOTIVATING THE CLIENT

Alcoholic individuals rarely seek out treatment on their own. They generally present for treatment only under threat of job loss, marital dissolution, loss of children or loss of friends, and, in some cases, threat of legal action. Even in the face of such negative contingencies, the individual who has not learned alternate ways of coping with difficult situations is apt to resist therapy. The following steps are included to enhance client motivation to engage in treatment and to modify his abuse of alcohol.

Treatment Deposits and Contracts

Treatment deposits consist of material objects of monetary and/or personal-sentimental value which are deposited with the worker against the client's premature termination from treatment or the client's abusing alcohol when abstinence or controlled drinking has been negotiated. For example, the client may deposit a sum of $200.00 which would be used towards payment of monetary penalties of $20.00 for the first failure, $40.00 for the second, $60.00 for the third and $80.00 for the fourth. Client termination without approval prior to attainment of treatment goals as agreed upon by the worker and client would result in loss of the full treatment deposit. Workers are encouraged to negotiate treatment deposits potent enough to inhibit client premature termination or abuse of alcohol. On the other hand, client desires to "lay everything on the line," "take my house, my car," are generally unrealistic insofar as they would likely not be acted on in the event of premature termination or alcohol abuse.

Contracting as a therapeutic tool has been described in Chapter 5. Contracts also serve to motivate clients and keep them in the treatment process.

Antabuse

As indicated in an earlier section Antabuse does not stand on its own as an effective treatment approach. However, Antabuse can provide strong support for the client who is motivated to succeed in treatment, is doubtful about his ability to maintain control over his drinking in the absence of Antabuse and is able and willing to take it according to schedule. Antabuse can foster client stability and thus, receptivity to treatment intervention at a level not possible in the face of continuing client inebriation.

Immediate Needs

Many clients, particularly, those from the lower and lower-middle socio-economic levels, present a variety of "down-to-earth" concerns at the outset of treatment. To foster a maximally stable environment, client housing, legal, and financial considerations should be addressed. It is unlikely that a client preoccupied with these concerns will be able to adequately participate in treatment efforts.

Bibliotherapy

Although reading materials do not stand alone as effective means of modifying alcohol abuse, for many, the written word has exceptional authority and can present a positive stimulus for change. *Drink to Your Health* by J. Adams [8] is one book which places alcohol and its use in balanced perspective. Chapter 2 provides an overview of the effect of excessive drinking on physical health. Miller and Munoz include a brief but comprehensive list of the negative consequences of excessive drinking in Appendix A of their book *How to Control Your Drinking* [9].

Readings of case reports of successfully treated clients (with names changed of course!) may foster additional optimism in the client who has a history of prior treatment failures or who is doubtful about achieving a successful treatment outcome.

Essay Assignments

The consequences of excessive drinking and the positive aspects of controlled drinking or abstinence may become more tangible through homework assignments. The client is asked to describe in clear terms at least five negative consequences for maintaining current drinking levels and at least five benefits of adopting controlling drinking practices or abstinence (depending on the client's treatment goal).

A parallel assignment could involve a brief personal history in which alcohol abuse has resulted in negative consequences.

Audiovisual Feedback

Feedback using videotape replays of drunken and sober behavior may also serve to highlight the negative effects of excessive drinking in social settings [10].

Involvement of Significant Others

Maintenance of adequate motivation is enhanced when individuals who are important to the client become involved in the treatment process. This is of obvious importance in the case of a married client whose spouse may be helping to maintain the client's excessive drinking in some manner. Friends and employers (see section on Industrial Alcohol Programs in Chapter 4) who are genuinely interested in client well-being may become strong sources of support. It is important to remember, nonetheless, that it is the *client* who must assume responsibility for his or her use of alcohol and not the supportive party.

Manipulation of Social Environment

Many problem drinkers have reduced their social interaction to a small group of friends or acquaintances who also have severe drinking problems. Hence, heavy use of alcohol becomes a requirement for maintaining such social relationships. Relapse into alcoholism by the treated individual is often associated with a return to the circle of alcoholic friends. Friends who abuse alcohol are better than no friends at all. Maintenance of treatment gains is enhanced when the client is encouraged to develop relationships with individuals who do not abuse alcohol and who would not tolerate it on the part of the client. Social skills development and/or social anxiety reduction may also need to be addressed if this type of social environment manipulation is to succeed.

The Alternatives Program for Drug Dependencies in Montreal and Vancouver, Canada, actually takes this concept one step further. Clients accepted into outpatient treatment are introduced to a group of three to ten program volunteers who donate their time to serving as alternate peers. The nature of such client-volunteer contacts is purely social and not counseling-oriented. After an introductory meeting volunteers and the client determine their interest in continuing to see each other socially; roughly half of such relationships do so. The client and volunteer often develop strong relationships and, not infrequently, the client comes to develop even stronger friendships with members of the volunteer's circle of friends than the volunteer himself. Community minded individuals, whether students, housewives, businessmen or laborers, etc., exist in each city. Such volunteer programs serve as important adjuncts to treatment and have proved satisfying to the volunteers involved.

GOAL SETTING

Based on a behavioral diagnosis [11] of information collected via the Personal History forms, the Continuous Data Questionnaire and other assessment devices, a number of alcohol and nonalcohol related treatment goals may be delineated.

The following steps are suggested:

1. Define each goal in terms of identifiable behaviors;
2. Define the goal in such a way that it is measurable in terms of frequency, quantity, or length of time;
3. Define the situations in which the desired behavior is to occur; the time, the place, with whom, how, the emotional state.

Some examples of behavioral goals are:

(a) to drink a maximum of two 12-ounce bottles of beer per 24-hour period, at a rate of no more than one bottle of beer per hour;

(b) to spend one hour per evening with the television off speaking with one's spouse without arguing;

(c) to make the acquaintance of three new people per week, to say "Hello" to them and to find out their names, phone numbers and two of their interests;

(d) to complete five applications for employment by 2:00 p.m. each weekday.

4. Determine *with the client* the relative importance of the treatment goals. Some clients may have 5–7 treatment goals defined. In order to determine the order in which the goals are to be addressed, it is most helpful to write each of treatment goals on an index card and have the client to do a card sort, identifying the priority of goals as he or she sees it. This is often an excellent yet simple way of determining those goals which the client feels most motivated to work on. Worker reservations about the ordering of the treatment goals should be aired and revisions of the priorities sought out with the client when indicated;

5. Determine baseline data as per "collection of baseline" (pre-treatment) data above;

6. Once the final treatment goals are defined, and baseline data collected, intermediate goals may be determined: my goal is to weigh 145 pounds in six months. I now weigh 185 pounds. Therefore, in one month my goal is

to weigh 175 pounds (weight to be determined on my home scales at 8:00 a.m. each day).

Once the intermediate goals are defined, treatment intervention may commence as per outlined in your assessment report (see Table 6.5). Continued gathering of data relevant to the treatment goals is necessary. In order to make a determination of the effectiveness of treatment, the client's performance is compared with the baseline that was established and the criterion of treatment success specified in the treatment goal. If the goal is not being achieved then the worker and the client may need to renegotiate treatment goal and/or treatment approach adopted.

TABLE 6.1
Michigan Alcoholism Screening Test (MAST)

Date Performed: _____

Interviewer: _____

Questions

*1. Do you feel you are a normal drinker?

2. Have you ever awakened the morning after some drinking the night before and found you could not remember a part of the evening before?

3. Does your wife/husband/parents ever worry or complain about your drinking?

*4. Can you stop drinking without a struggle after one or two drinks?

5. Do you ever feel bad about your drinking?

*6. Do friends or relatives think you are a normal drinker?

7. Do you every try to limit your drinking to certain times of the day or to certain places?

*8. Are you always able to stop drinking when you want to?

9. Have you ever attended a meeting of A.A.?

10. Has drinking ever created a problem with you and wife/husband?

11. Have you gotten into fights when drinking?

12. Has your wife/husband/family member ever gone to anyone for help about your drinking?

13. Have you ever lost friends or girlfriends/boyfriends because of drinking?

14. Have you ever gotten into trouble at work because of drinking?

15. Have you ever lost a job because of drinking?

16. Have you ever neglected your obligations, your family, or your work for two or more days in a row, because of your drinking?

17. Do you ever drink before noon?

18. Have you ever been told you have liver trouble, (cirrhosis)?

19. Have you ever had D.T.s, severe shaking, heard voices or seen things that weren't there, after heavy drinking?

20. Have you ever gone to anyone for help about your drinking?

21. Have you ever been in a hospital because of drinking?

22. Have you ever been a patient in a psychiatric hospital or on a psychiatric ward of a general hospital where drinking was part of the problem?

23. Have you ever been seen at a psychiatric or mental health clinic, or gone to a doctor, social worker or clergyman for help with an emotional problem in which drinking had played a part?

24. Have you ever been arrested, even for a few hours, because of drunk behavior?

25. Have you ever been arrested for drunk driving or driving after drinking?

TABLE 6.2
Client Personal History
To be completed by client at clinic. To be given once during Assessment.

Date Administered _____

Administered by _____

Instructions to Client

Your answers to the following questions are needed to assist us in planning your treatment program. Please try to answer each question as accurately as possible. If you have trouble understanding any question, feel free to ask for further information.

IDENTIFYING INFORMATION.

1) Name of Client _____

2) Home address _____

   Phone _____

3) Name and address of person through whom you can always be reached.

   _____

   _____ Phone _____

4) Employer _____ Phone _____ Address _____

   Doctor _____ Phone _____ Address _____

   Probation/Parole Officer _____ Phone _____

   Address _____

   Lawyer _____ Phone _____ Address _____

EDUCATIONAL HISTORY

1) What schools or universities have you attended?

Name	Location	# yrs. completed	Age of Leaving	Reason for leaving
_____	_____	_____	_____	_____
_____	_____	_____	_____	_____
_____	_____	_____	_____	_____

Additional Special Training

_____	_____	_____	_____	_____
_____	_____	_____	_____	_____

2) How well did you get along with fellow students?

3) How well did you get along with your teachers?

VOCATIONAL HISTORY

1) What jobs have you had? Begin with most recent.

Position	Employer	Length of stay	Reason for Leaving
_____	_____	_____	_____
_____	_____	_____	_____
_____	_____	_____	_____

2) How many different jobs have you had in the last year? _____

3) How much does it cost you to live? (average/month)

Rent _____

Mortgage _____

Food _____

Utilities _____

Clothes _____

Leisure activities _____

Other _____

Total _____

HEALTH HISTORY

1) How was your health during childhood/adolescence?

2) Have any of your illnesses been alcohol related (include psychiatric)?

3) Were you hospitalized for any of these illnesses?

4) Please list any surgical operations and age at time.

5) Please list any accidents and age at time.

6) When were you last examined by a doctor? What doctor?

7) Underline any of the following that apply to you.

headaches	financial problems	no appetite
heart trouble	dizziness	alcoholism
nightmares	stomach trouble	shy with people
fell tense	tired	can't make decisions
depressed	take sedatives	home conditions bad
unable to relax	feel panicky	concentration
can't make friends	suicidal ideas	difficulties
sexual problems	can't keep a job	can't sleep
overambitious	inferiority feelings	other
memory problems	fainting spells	
don't like weekends or vacations		
unable to have a good time		

8) Menstrual History (Female only)

a) age at first period?

   b) did you know about menstruation or was it unexpected?

   c) do you have cramps?

   d) date of last period?

   e) do your periods affect your moods?

9) Have you had any abortions or miscarriages? (Female only)

SIGNIFICANT OTHERS

A. *Friends and family*

   1) Write a brief description of the nature and closeness of your past and present relationships with your friends and family.

   a) past:

   b) present:

   2) Are any of your friends/family alcohol abusers?

   3) Are any of them *not* alcohol abusers?

   4) What was it like at home while you were growing up? Describe how your parents got along with each other and with the children.

   5) In what ways were you punished by your parents as a child?

   6) If your parents are no longer together explain what happened and why.

   7) If you weren't brought up by your parents, who did bring you up and between what years?

   8) If you have a step-parent, how old were you when your parents remarried?

   9) Has any other relative had an important influence on you? If so, describe who and in what way.

   10) Has any member of your family had psychiatric treatment? If so, please describe when, for what reason, for how long and the outcome.

   11) Is there any other information about your family that you think is important?

B. *Partner* (Spouse or Common-law)

   1) Client's marital status: _____ single _____ widowed _____ divorced
   _____ separated _____ married or common-law

   2) Have you been married or lived common-law before? If yes, give details.
   If not married or common-law, skip to section C *"Children."*

   3) Date of marriage or time you moved in together (current spouse/common-law partner).

   4) How long did you know your partner before living together?

   5) Do you plan to stay with this person? If not, for what reasons?

   6) Describe the personality of your partner in your own words.

   7) In what ways do you get along?

   8) In what ways don't you get along?

   9) Do you share activities with your partner? What activities and how often?

10) Which one of these activities do you enjoy doing the most?

11) Does he/she go out with other men/women? How do you feel about it?

12) Do you or did you drink heavily together? Who started first?

C. *Children*

1) Do you have any children? _____ yes _____ no

2) If yes, please list name, sex and age.
   If no children, skip to the next section—"*Contact with Previous Agencies.*"

Name	Sex	Age

3) Where are your children living now? With whom?

4) How are they being supported?

5) Have you had any children with your present husband, wife or common-law partner?

6) Have you adopted any of your husband, wife, or common-law partner's children?

7) Do any of your children present special problems to you?

CONTACT WITH PREVIOUS AGENCIES

1) In the table below list other rehabilitation programs, agencies or professionals, etc. that you have contacted or are presently in contact with in relation to your alcohol or psychiatric problems.

List the six most important beginning with the most recent.

In *Column one* list type of treatment, name of place or person and approximate dates and length of treatment.

In *Column two* list reasons for treatment, and whether or not you found treatment on your own.

In *Column three* state why you left treatment and if you think you gained from it. Why or why not.

Treatment	Reasons	Results	Release Form
Place/person	Found on own,	Reasons for	Requested Received
Type of Treatment	yes, no	leaving	(for agency use)
Approx. date	Reasons	Did you gain from	
Length		it? yes, no	

1.

2.

3.

4.

5.

6.

2) Were you referred to the clinic by a doctor or other professional person?

_____ Yes _____ No (If yes, specify whom) _____
　　　　　　　　　　　　　　　　　　　　　　　　　　(Name)

_____　　　　_____
　　　(Title or Position)　　　　　　*(Building Title, clinic, dept., etc.)*

_____
　　　　(Street Address or Box No.)

_____　　　　_____
　　　(City or Town)　　　　　　　　　　*(Province)*

Telephone: _____ _____
　　　　　　(Area)　　*(Number)*

JUDICIAL HISTORY

1) Have you ever been convicted of any criminal offences?

_____ Yes _____ No

2) If yes, complete the following tables using the codes furnished:
(If no, skip to next section "*Motivation for Treatment*")

Code for Resulting Action	*Code if you were Incarcerated*
A. Sentence suspended	A. Juvenile home
B. Fined	B. Jail
C. Probation	C. Penitentiary
D. Sentence pending 　 Appeal pending	
E. Incarcerated	
F. Parole	

Charge	Date of Conviction	Resulting Action	Where	If Incarcerated Dates	Paroled Yes/No	Broke Parole Yes/No

MOTIVATION FOR TREATMENT

1) In your own words, how would you define alcohol abuse?

2) Would you say that you abuse alcohol?   _____ Yes
                                            _____ No

3) On your own, and without outside agency help, what steps have you taken in an attempt to stop abusing alcohol?

4) Some people say that alcohol abuse is like a bad habit that you learn. Do you agree?

5) In your own words, why is it important that you stop abusing alcohol?

6) What good do you hope to get from therapy?

7) What things would like to do after you have stopped abusing alcohol?

8) What is likely to help you maintain a lifestyle not involving alcohol abuse?

TABLE 6.3
Behavioral Assessment of Alcohol Abuse

To be completed by the client at the clinic with the therapist. To be given once only at the start of treatment.

BEVERAGE PREFERENCES

Card Sort Instructions:

Now, I am going to give you a set of cards (for beverage types, see list on last page), with various kinds of alcohol beverages printed on them. Here, we are interested in getting an idea of what your favorite drinks would be, if you were in the mood for drinking.

a)   First, I want you to look at the cards, to get an idea of the overall selection. Then, I want you to sort the cards into two piles: place those cards in a pile on the left, if they list a beverage which you would *like to drink*, if you were in the mood to drink and were given a free choice of selection. Pay no attention to the price or availability of each drink; we want your *ideal* preferences for drinks—as if you had a choice to select whatever you wanted from a liquor store, without worrying about money.

Put the cards in a pile on the right if they list a beverage which you *do not like to drink*, when you are given a free choice of selection. Any questions? All right, begin sorting the cards.

(Wait until first sorting is complete)

Now I want you to take the pile on the left, and arrange the cards in order of your favorite choices. Put the one card on the top which lists your most *favorite beverage*, if you had a free choice of what to drink. Then sort the rest of the cards to represent your second, third, and fourth choices, and so on through the pile. The card on the bottom should list your least preferred choice.

(Indicate the ordering of preferences. Then take the *first three* preferred beverages, and obtain the favorite *brand*, if any, and the *manner* in which the subject prefers to drink each, i.e., with or without mixer, ice, etc. Specify brand names if possible, for mixers. List this information immediately below).

(i)   First Choice Beverage: _____ Brand: _____

      Preferred Manner of Drinking: _____

(ii) Second Choice: _____ Brand: _____

      Preferred Manner of Drinking _____

(iii) Third Choice: _____ Brand: _____

      Preferred Manner of Drinking _____

(iv) Other beverages of choice, in order: _____ _____

b)   OK, now I want you to go through all the cards a second time. First, I want you to again sort the cards into two piles: place those cards in a pile on the left, if they list a beverage which *you actually do drink*, from time to time. For many people, the drink they would pick as their *favorite* beverage may not be the one they actually drink the most, due to reasons of cost and so forth. So, put those cards in the left pile which lists beverages which you actually do drink in more or less amounts on different occasions. Put those cards in a pile on the right if they list a beverage which you *never* have drunk, as far as you can remember. Any questions? All right, begin sorting the cards.

(Wait until this sorting is complete)

Secondly, I want you to take the pile on the left, and arrange the cards in order of how frequently or how often you drink each beverage. Put the one card on the top which lists the beverage which you actually drink the most of all. Then sort the rest of the cards to represent which beverage you drink second most often, third most often, and so on, through out the pile. The card on the bottom should list the beverage which you drink least frequently of all.

(Indicate the ordering of cards. Then take the *first three* most frequently consumed beverages, and ascertain the *brand* most frequently consumed, and the preferred manner of drinking, as before. List this information immediately below.)

(i) Most frequently Consumed Drink: _____ Brand: _____

Preferred Manner of Drinking _____

(ii) Second Beverage: _____ Brand: _____

Preferred Manner of Drinking _____

(iii) Third Beverage: _____ Brand: _____

Preferred Manner of Drinking: _____

(iv) Other beverages consumed, by order: _____

_____

EFFECTS OF DRINKING

Card Sort Instructions:

We are interested in knowing more about what kinds of effects alcohol has on you. I am going to give you another set of cards with different possible effects written on them. I would like you to sort these cards into two piles. Place those cards in a pile on the left, if they describe effects that alcohol has on you when you are actually drinking. Put the cards in a pile on the right which lists effects which *you do not get* from alcohol when you are drinking. Any questions? All, begin sorting the cards.

Positive Effects *Tension Reduction*	*Negative Feelings:* *Anger/Frustration*	*Negative Feelings:* *Anxiety*
_____Happy	_____Anger	_____Afraid
_____Relaxed	_____Sad	_____Nervous
_____Peaceful	_____Depressed	_____Tense
_____Calm	_____Lonely	_____Excited
_____Unafraid	_____Frustrated	_____Restless

Postive Feelings: *Socially outgoing and Positive Self-esteem*	*Negative Feelings:* *Socially Withdrawn and Negative Self-esteem*
_____Secure	_____Insecure
_____Superior	_____Inferior
_____Outgoing	_____Withdrawn
_____Friendly	_____Unfriendly
_____Strong	_____Weak

(Spread out chosen list of effects in front of subject)

Now, looking at these cards you have chosen, I want you to pick out the *five* cards which represent the five most accurate descriptions of effects which are true for you when you are drinking. (Wait until subject picks the five cards). O.K., now would you please arrange these five cards in order from the most true effect for you to the least true effect of the five cards. Put the one card listing the most true effect on top, and the card with the least true effect on the bottom, with the other three cards arranged in the middle in terms of how accurately they describe the effects which you get from drinking. Any questions?

(List the five cards in order of accuracy, below)

Comments, if any: _____

1. _____   _____

2. _____   _____

3. _____   _____

4. _____   _____

5. _____   _____

HISTORY OF ALCOHOL USE

A. *Development of Alcohol Abuse Problem*

1. How were you introduced to alcohol?

    1) through friends
    2) through acquaintances
    3) through spouse (includes common-law)
    4) through brother or sister
    5) through parents
    6) by myself
    7) other: (specify) _____

2. Approximately how old were you when you first drank alcohol? _____

3. Do you remember what type of alcohol you drank at that time?

4. Describe the feelings you experienced and the situation (surroundings) that you were in at the time of your first experience.

5. Approximately how old were you when alcohol became a "real problem" for you; that is, when it began to have an effect on your life which you did not really approve of? _____ Age

    _____ Denies that it is a real problem.

    At that particular time in your life, when alcohol first became a real problem, were there any special circumstances or events which occurred which you feel were responsible for it becoming a problem? (If yes, summarize circumstances): _____

    _____

6. How would you describe the general alcohol use of each of your parents?

    Which category best suits your father (or guardian), and your mother?

Father	*Mother*
_____Not applicable	_____Not applicable
_____Nonuser (abstinent)	_____Nonuser (abstinent)
_____Occasional user	_____Occasional user
_____Moderate or average user	_____Moderate or average user
_____Frequent or heavy	_____Frequent or heavy
_____Alcohol abuse	_____Alcohol abuse

Type of Alcohol: Type of Alcohol:

_____   _____

Comments: _____

_____

B. *Current Pattern of Alcohol Abuse*

   1. Who do you drink with? List three in order of importance:

      1) _____
      2) _____
      3) _____

      1) alone
      2) with friends
      3) with acquaintances
      4) with partner (includes common-law)
      5) with parents
      6) other: specify _____

   2. Where are you most often drunk? List the three most frequent places:

      1) _____
      2) _____
      3) _____

      1) in the street
      2) at work
      3) in bars
      4) at friend's home
      5) at parties
      6) at school
      7) at home
      8) other: specify _____

   3. When are you most drunk?

      time of month _____
      days of week _____
      time of day _____
      weekends only? _____
      evenings only? _____

   4. After drinking heavily, have you ever had any of the following experiences? If yes, please circle the number.

      1) shakes
      2) nausea or vomiting
      3) delirium tremens
      4) anxiety/restlessness
      5) blackout/memory lapse
      6) convulsions or seizures

        Is there anything else that happens to you after drinking heavily?

        If yes, specify: _____

5. In your opinion has drinking heavily been the cause of any of the following events in your life? (Check for positive reply)

_____Losing a job or jobs
_____Getting arrested
_____Becoming divorced or separated
_____Losing a personal friend or friends
_____Being broke or owing people money
_____Having a serious medical problem (specify)_____

6. Since alcohol first became a real problem for you, have you ever had a period(s) when you have abstained? _____ yes _____ no. If yes, please complete the table below:

Dates	Length of Time	Reason(s) for Stopping	Reason(s) for starting again

7. Usual Drinking Pattern

What would you say best describes your overall drinking habits? Would you say that you were a *periodic, intermittent drinker* (one who drinks heavily on a binge or drinking bout every so often, with periods of little or no drinking binges), or a *steady, regular drinker* (one who continuously drinks more or less the same amount on a day-to-day basis)?

_____ Periodic _____ Steady _____ Cannot say
(or both)

a) *Section for Periodic Drinkers and Cannot Say Group*

About how many drinking bouts have you had in the past six months?

_____

About how long does your average drinking bout usually last?

_____ hours _____ days

What is the longest bout you have ever had?

_____ hours _____days

On the average, how much time goes by between drinking bouts?

_____ days _____ weeks _____ months

How would you describe the circumstances which mark the end of one of these drinking bouts? That is, what factors determine when you finally *stop* drinking? _____

b) *Section for Steady Drinkers and Cannot Say Group*

Are there any particular days of the week during which you drink more than on other days?_____ yes_____ no (list days if yes):

_____

8. Factors Associated with Drinking

1. Do you sometimes take a drink in the morning, before breakfast?
_____ yes _____ no

2. Do you find that you are unable to stop drinking, once you have had one or two drinks on any occasion? _____ yes _____ no

If yes: Why do you think you are unable to stop after the first one or two drinks? _____

REASONS FOR ALCOHOL ABUSE

Card sort instructions:

People abuse alcohol for a variety of reasons. I am going to give you a set of cards with various problems printed on them. I want you to sort the cards into two piles. Place those cards on the left which describe problems you are experiencing; place the other cards in a pile on the right. Please be sure to indicate to me problems that are not listed but which are pertinent to your abuse of alcohol.

1. Referring to the above, what is the *main reason* why you abuse alcohol?

2. Are there any other reasons why you drink which you consider important? If yes, what are they?

3. Do you have any inner thoughts (i.e., about failure, being rejected, etc.) or emotional feelings (tension, anger, grief, anxiety, depression, etc.), or things *within you* as a person, which "trigger" your need or desire to drink at a particular moment in time?

4. Are there any particular situations or set of events, things which happen to you in the *outside world*, which could be *most* likely to make you feel like drinking?

5. Can you describe a situation or set of events which would be *least likely* to make you feel like drinking? In other words, when do you *least* feel like drinking?

6. When you are *actually drinking*, what, for you, is the most positive or desirable effect? In other words, what is the thing you like *best* about alcohol? (Probe: Any other positive effects?)

7. When you are *actually drinking*, what, for you, is the most negative or undesirable effect? In other words, what is the thing you like *least* about alcohol? (Probe: Any other negative effects?)

EMOTIONAL HISTORY

1. State in your own words the kind of problems, including nonalcohol related, you have and how long you've had them. Indicate how and when they developed.

2. How bad are your present problems? (circle one)

   1) midly upsetting
   2) moderately upsetting
   3) very severe
   4) extremely severe
   5) totally incapacitating

3. List your five main fears:

   1)
   2)
   3)
   4)
   5)

4. List any situations that make you feel anxious.

5. List any situations that make you feel calm and relaxed.

6. Do you lose control often? (e.g. temper, crying, fighting) If so please describe.

7. Please complete the following self-description:

I am _____

I am _____

I am _____

I am _____

I feel _____

I feel _____

I feel _____

I feel _____

I think _____

I think _____

I think _____

I think _____

I wish _____

I wish _____

I wish _____

I wish _____

8. How would you be described:

   a) by yourself:

   b) by your partner (married or common law):

   c) by your best friend:

   d) by someone who dislikes you:

SEXUAL HISTORY

1. Are you heterosexual, homosexual or bisexual?

2. Is your present sex life satisfactory? If not, please describe nature of sexual difficulties.

3. Describe any important details about your first or other sexual experiences.

4. Did you ever feel guilty or anxious about sex or masturbation? If yes, please explain.

Beverage List (for card sort)

Blended Whiskey

Bourbon

Brandy

Gin

Rum

Scotch Whiskey

Tequila

Vodka

Liqueur

Beer and/or Ale

Malt Liquor

Red Dry Wine

Red Sweet Wine

White Dry Wine

White Sweet Wine

Sparkling Wine or Champagne

Special Fortified Wine (20% alcohol)

Nonbeverage Alcohol (shaving lotion)

Other (Specify): _____

Reasons for Alcohol Abuse

insomnia

headaches

chronic physical pain

anxiety

recent death, divorce, separation

inferiority feelings

can't make decisions

depression

can't relax

can't make friends

problems on the job

wrong career choice

educational problems

marital problems

sexual dysfunction

homosexuality

dating relations

being taken advantage of

communication problems

problems with children

boredom

avoiding tough problems

dishonesty

criminal activity

can't have a good time

friends are alcoholic

overweight

money problems

religion

lack of recreational outlets

failure to achieve desired goals

unusual thoughts

loneliness

guilt

rejection by others

unpleasant memories

aggression

other (specify)

TABLE 6.4
Continuous Data Questionnaire

To be completed by therapist in interview with the client. To be given: (1) during assessment, (2) at the start of treatment, and following that, (3), at regular three month intervals, and lastly, (4) at treatment completion (or termination). Following treatment completion, the CDQ will be given as a follow-up at three, six, and twelve month periods in post completion (or termination) of therapy. Report periods are defined as follows:

The first time the questionnaire is given is during the Assessment period. In all interviews, the questions are asked with respect to the previous three months of the client's life (or the period since the last CDQ, if that is less than three months). Thus the words "report period" in this questionnaire refer to the previous three months of the client's life. Please give responses to all questions, even is the answer is zero.

Name of Client _____

1. Stage of Treatment:

   1. Assessment
   2. Treatment initiation
   3. Treatment
   4. Treatment completion

   5. Follow-up (not in treatment,
              not yet discharged)
   6. Completed program (discharged)
   7. Terminated, explain
   8. Readmitted

2. Date administered _____
   Administered by _____

I. ALCOHOL USE

Regardless of treatment goal (abstinence or controlled drinking), answer the following as completely and as accurately as you can:

1. Over the past three months you have consumed alcohol on the average as follows:

   a. how much per week?
   b. how many days per week?
   c. how many days abstinent per week?
   d. amount per day?
   e. preference of beverage a) _____ b) _____ c) _____
   f. who with?
   g. where?
   h. note all other drugs taken whether licit or illicit include prescription and over the counter medications

2. Most of my friends are _____. My spouse (including common-law) is _____ (place correct number in blank space).

   1) abstainers
   2) occasional users
   3) moderate or average users
   4) frequent or heavy users
   5) alcoholics
   6) not applicable

3. During the past report period what is the longest period of time over which you did not drink?

   Days _____ Weeks _____ Months _____ Always drank _____

4. How difficult is it for you to control the amount of alcohol that you consume?

1) extremely easy
2) moderately easy
3) neither difficult or easy
4) moderately difficult
5) extremely difficult

5. During the past report period your alcohol urges have been:

1) nil or almost none
2) quite weak
3) average
4) moderately strong
5) very strong

6. When do you drink?

A.
1) weekends only
2) during week
3) both
4) N/A

B.
1) morning mostly
2) afternoon mostly
3) evening mostly
4) at any time
5) N/A

7. General comment on drug-alcohol use (thoughts, feelings, attitudes, performance)

II. WORK-EDUCATION

1. Are you employed _____ Not employed _____

2. Has your place of employment changed since last report period? Yes _____ No _____. If yes, how many times? _____ If not employed proceed to #9.

Name of employer (if changed since last report)_____

Name and address of firm or company_____

_____

Telephone_____

3. Average monthly income from this job (indicate to nearest dollar)

$ _____ None _____

4. Length of time in present job.

Years _____ Months _____ Weeks _____

5. How many days have you missed from work during this report period?

a. Alcohol-related _____
b. Illness_____
c. Leave of absence_____

6. How many times were you late for work in the last month? _____

7. How satisfied are you with your job?

1) Very satisfied
2) Moderately satisfied
3) Neither satisfied nor unsatisfied
4) Moderately unsatisfied
5) Very unsatisfied
6) N/A

8. How would you rate yourself on your performance at work?

   1) Excellent
   2) Quite good
   3) Average
   4) Moderately poor
   5) Very poor
   6) N/A

9. Length of time unemployed. Yrs. _____ Months _____ Weeks _____

10. Usual occupational status.

    1) Full-time (more than six hours per day)
    2) Part-time (less than six hours per day)
    3) Temporarily unemployed
    4) Permanently unemployed
    5) Welfare

11. Usual occupational category.

    1) Professional, executive, or managerial
    2) White collar (secretary, clerk, etc.)
    3) Skilled labourer, tradesman (chef, electrician)
    4) Unskilled labourer
    5) Semi-professional (nurse, skilled technician)
    6) Houseperson
    7) Unemployed
    8) Student
    9) Other

    Also, please indicate the specific job title. _____

12. Additional Income other than job if employed (during report period) 1) welfare, 2) unemployment, 3) donations, 4) loans, 5) illegal sources, 6) personal wealth, 7) spouse/commonlaw partner, 8) family, 9) other, specify.

    Source _____ Amount _____

    Source _____ Amount _____

    Source _____ Amount _____

13. How much money do you presently owe?

    mortgage _____
    car debts _____
    credit cards _____
    family _____
    friends _____
    others _____   _____

14. How much money have you repaid on loans, etc. (during this report period)?

    mortgage _____
    car debts _____
    credit cards _____
    family _____
    friends _____
    others _____

15. Have you been meeting required payments? Yes _____ No _____

16. Do you plan to continue your education or training?

    1) am currently doing so
    2) yes, most definitely
    3) yes, want to
    4) maybe, thinking about it
    5) undecided
    6) no plans
    7) never

    If #1 or #2, specify _____

17. General comments on work-education-income areas (thoughts, feelings, attitudes, etc.)

III. FAMILY INVOLVEMENT

1. Who do you live with? (use up to three categories)

	Now	Usually
1) Spouse/common law partner	_____	_____
2) Parents	_____	_____
3) Grandparents	_____	_____
4) Brother or sister		
5) Other relatives		
6) Friends		
7) By yourself		
8) institution or at a residence		
9) members of the same commune		

2. Main type of place that you live in:

    1) no regular place (street, abandoned bldg., etc.)
    2) hostel, rooming or boarding house
    3) hotel
    4) apartment or other family dwelling
    5) jail, prison, or other correctional institution
    6) therapeutic community or other rehabilitation facility
    7) hospital
    8) school, college, or university residence
    9) employers housing, including armed forces
    10) own house
    11) other, specify _____

3. How well do you get along with your family? _____ (other than spouse)
                          friends? _____
            spouse (incl. common-law)? _____

    1) very well
    2) moderately well
    3) neither well nor poorly
    4) moderately poor
    5) very poor
    6) N/A

4. How often do you do things with your family? _____ (other than spouse)
   friends? _____
   spouse (incl. common-law)? _____
   alone? _____
   1) very often (every day)
   2) quite often (several times/week)
   3) sometimes (several times/month
   4) rarely (several times/year)
   5) never
   6) N/A

5. How important are your friends to you? _____
   family? _____ (other than spouse)
   spouse (incl. common-law)? _____
   1) very important
   2) moderately important
   3) neither important nor unimportant
   4) moderately unimportant
   5) very unimportant
   6) N/A

6. How important do you feel that you are to your spouse? _____ (incl. common-
   friends? _____   law)
   (other than spouse) family? _____
   1) very important
   2) moderately important
   3) neither important nor unimportant
   4) moderately unimportant
   5) very unimportant
   6) N/A

7. How well do you handle arguments with your spouse? _____ (incl. common-law)
   family? _____ (other than spouse)
   friends? _____
   1) very constructively
   2) moderately well
   3) neither well nor poorly
   4) moderately poorly
   5) very poorly
   6) ignore the problem
   7) don't argue (probe)
   8) N/A

8. Do you usually keep appointments, dates and obligations to your
   friends? _____
   family? _____ (other than spouse)
   spouse? _____ (incl. common-law)
   1) yes, always
   2) usually
   3) sometimes
   4) rarely
   5) almost never
   6) N/A

9. General comments on family involvement (thoughts, feelings, attitudes, performance, etc.)

IV. SOCIAL-RECREATIONAL-COMMUNITY INVOLVEMENT

1. What were your social/recreational activities during the past report period? (Include informal activities like drinking with friends) (Indicate if any of these were new.)

Activities   *New (Yes, No)*

_____   _____

_____   _____

_____   _____

_____   _____

_____   _____

2. About how many times a week do you participate in these social/recreational activities?

1) four or more
2) two to three times
3) once a week
4) less than once
5) rarely or never

3. During the past report period, how many new friends have you met by participating in these events?

1) none
2) one friend
3) two friends
4) three friends
5) four friends
6) five or more friends

4. General comments on social-recreational-community involvement (thoughts, feelings, attitudes, performance).

V. JUDICIAL INVOLVEMENT

1. During this report period, has there been any change (less or more involvement) in your status with the criminal justice system?

Yes _____ No _____

** If "yes," complete judicial section, if "no" skip to Personality & Emotional Development.

2. Reasons for arrests during report period. Record number of arrests in each category (use zero where appropriate).

	Number
1) Crimes against person, e.g. assault, rape, homicide	_____
2) Crimes for profit, e.g. robbery, burglary, forgery, theft	_____
3) Prostitution, pimping, or soliciting	_____
4) Gambling	_____
5) Motor vehicle driving offences (excluding minor offences)	_____
6) Other, specify	_____

3. If arrested during report period please indicate charge, conviction and sentence.

charge _____
conviction _____
sentence _____

charge _____
conviction _____
sentence _____

charge _____
conviction _____
sentence _____

charge _____
conviction _____
sentence _____

4. Do you have any outstanding bench warrants?

Yes _____   No _____

If yes, specify _____

5. Is there a presentence report outstanding?

Yes _____   No _____

6. Has there been a change towards less involvement with the criminal justice system (i.e., off parole, off probation, cleared bench warrant?) Yes _____ No _____

If yes, specify _____

7. General comments (thoughts, attitudes, feelings, performance, etc.).

VI. PERSONALITY AND EMOTIONAL DEVELOPMENT

1. Please rate the following characteristics as you feel they may apply to you.

    1) very low
    2) moderately low
    3) neither high nor low
    4) moderately high
    5) very high

    1) responsibility to self _____.
    2) Responsibility to others _____.
    3) Self-esteem (self-worth) _____.
    4) Initiative (motivation) _____.
    5) Anxiety _____.
    6) Sociability _____.
    7) Assertiveness _____.
    8) General feeling of well-being _____.
    9) Hostility-aggression-punishment towards others _____.
    10) Depression _____.

2. Please indicate on each of these scales, how you felt during the report period. (circle correct number)

   1) tense   1 2 3 4 5   relaxed
   2) tolerant   1 2 3 4 5   critical
   3) depressed   1 2 3 4 5   happy
   4) hard (tough) 1 2 3 4 5   soft (tender)
   5) calm   1 2 3 4 5   nervous
   6) sickly   1 2 3 4 5   healthy
   7) forgiving   1 2 3 4 5   unforgiving
   8) sociable   1 2 3 4 5   unsociable
   9) unfriendly   1 2 3 4 5   friendly

3. Comments or reflections on personality and moods.

VII. HEALTH

1. Your overall physical health has been: _____.Your overall mental health has been: _____.

   1) excellent
   2) very good
   3) average
   4) poor
   5) very poor

2. During the past report period, have you had any major diseases or illnesses? Yes _____ No _____

   If yes, specify

3. Have you been eating regular meals?

   1) all of the time
   2) most of the time
   3) occasionally
   4) rarely or never

4. Have you been eating reasonably balanced or nutritious meals? (Probe what they have eaten over the last few days.) Answer to be rated by therapist.

   1) all of the time
   2) most of the time
   3) occasionally
   4) rarely or never

5. On the average, how many hours of sleep do you get each night?

   1) more than 10 hours   4) 5-6 hours
   2) 9-10 hours   5) less than 5 hours
   3) 7-8 hours

6. Is that enough? Yes _____ No _____

7. Do you use drugs/alcohol to help get to sleep? Yes _____ No _____

8. How much time do you spend doing physical exercise? (sports, work, bicycling, etc.)

   1) more than fifteen hours per week
   2) ten to fifteen hours per week
   3) five to ten hours per week

    4) one to five hours per week
    5) less than one hour a week

9. Have you had any difficulties with menstruation?

    Yes _____ No _____ N/A _____

    If yes, specify. _____

10. During the past report period how many times did you see a medical doctor? _____
    Psychiatrist? _____

11. How much time have you spent (during this report period) in the hospital for
    physical reasons? _____ Mental reasons? _____

    1) no time
    2) less than one day (not overnite)
    3) one day to less than one week
    4) one week to two weeks
    5) two weeks to less than a month
    6) one month to three months
    7) three to six months
    8) more than six months

12. Have you attempted to harm yourself during the report period?

    No _____ Yes _____

    (During Assessment, check for anytime in client history.) If yes, how many times have you
    attempted to harm yourself (including attempted suicide) and by what method. Please
    indicate approximate date(s).

    SEXUAL HEALTH

1. Your sexual drive or urges are:

    1) strong
    2) average
    3) weak
    4) very weak
    5) no urges

2. Can you reach orgasm through intercourse, masturbation, or other means?

    1) all of the time
    2) most of the time
    3) occasionally
    4) seldom
    5) never

3. How satisfied are you with your sex life?

    1) very satisfied
    2) moderately satisfied
    3) neither satisfied nor unsatisfied
    4) moderately unsatisfied
    5) very unsatisfied

4. General comments, thoughts, attitudes, etc. on general or sexual health.

VIII. MOTIVATION

1. What do you see as the most desirable goals of treatment here for you? And, giving your honest opinion, how well do you feel that you have achieved (i.e. your present success) or will achieve these goals (i.e. your expected success)?

   1) very successful
   2) moderately successful
   3) no indication (haven't attempted, no indication of success yet, etc.)
   4) moderately unsuccessful
   5) very unsuccessful
   6) N/A (no goals)

Goals	*Present Success*	*Expected Success*
1. _____	_____	_____
2. _____	_____	_____
3. _____	_____	_____
4. _____	_____	_____

2. How important is it for you to stop abusing alcohol or abstain?

   1) very important
   2) moderately important
   3) undecided
   4) moderately unimportant
   5) very unimportant

3. What do you feel would be your most desirable use of alcohol?

   1) never use
   2) use rarely
   3) use socially
   4) occasional heavy use (i.e. binge drinking)

4. Rate your responses to the following items:

   1) strongly agree
   2) agree
   3) undecided
   4) disagree
   5) strongly disagree

   A. My alcohol problem is something I can get over soon. _____
   B. No one I know is really interested in my problem. _____
   C. Nowadays a person has to live pretty much for today and let tomorrow take care of itself. _____
   D. I have a good relationship with all my family. _____
   E. It's hardly fair to bring children into the world with the way things look for the future. _____

   To be completed by interviewer

5. Interviewer's rating of person's overall motivation.

   1) very motivated
   2) moderately motivated

　　3) neither motivated nor unmotivated
　　4) moderately unmotivated
　　5) very unmotivated

6. Interviewer's expectancy of client success at decreasing/eliminating alcohol abuse.

　　1) very successful
　　2) moderately successful
　　3) neither successful nor unsuccessful
　　4) moderately unsuccessful
　　5) very unsuccessful

7. General comments, attitudes, feelings, thoughts, performance, etc. on motivation.

IX. THERAPIST'S SECTION

To be completed on second and subsequent administration of the Follow Up Questionnaire

1. Problems experienced during the Report Period which involved any of the following (circle yes or no)

1) Family	Yes	No
2) Friends	Yes	No
3) Drugs	Yes	No
4) Alcohol	Yes	No
5) Legal Authorities	Yes	No
6) School	Yes	No
7) Work	Yes	No
8) Finances	Yes	No
9) Health (include pregnancy)	Yes	No

　　If yes, explain briefly _____

　　_____

　　_____

　　_____

　　_____

2. Treatment facilities to which client was referred during Report Period, in order of occurrence

　　1) Inpatient (hospital)
　　2) Therapeutic community or other residence for group living (Initiation)
　　3) Partial hospitalization (day or night hospital)
　　4) Out patient
　　5) Other; specify_____
　　6) None

　　1) _____
　　2) _____
　　3) _____

3. Number of days client received therapeutic or support contacts at clinic _____

4. Where did therapeutic or support contacts occur? (list category letters in order or frequency with *most frequent* first

1) Hospital
2) Therapeutic community or other residence for group living
3) Day or night hospital
4) Outpatient clinic
5) Pharmacy
6) Vocational counselling or taining center
7) Social rehabilitation center
8) Religious organization
9) Patient's home
10) Community meeting place
11) Social or community agency
12) Other, specify_____

	Category	Agency Name
1)		
2)		
3)		
4)		
5)		

5. Drugs prescribed or administered to the client during the Report Period. Specify drugs used within each category. Check whether drugs used for withdrawal, maintenance or support.

	Withdrawal	Support	Maintenance
1) Antabuse			
2) Antidepressants			
3) Barbiturates or sedatives			
4) Tranquilizers			
5) Others, including those for medical conditions, Specify: _____			

6. Types of therapy or support received (circle Yes or No)

1) Vocational counselling	Yes	No
2) Vocational training	Yes	No
3) Educational training	Yes	No
4) Individual counselling	Yes	No
5) Group counselling	Yes	No
6) Family counselling	Yes	No
7) Recreational therapy	Yes	No
8) Therapeutic community or other living group	Yes	No
9) Religious activities	Yes	No
10) Other: Specify_____	Yes	No

7. Contacts with therapeutic or support personnel during Report Period.

1) Medical practitioner, western trained	Yes	No
2) Medical practitioner, indigenous	Yes	No
3) Specialist in psychiatry	Yes	No
4) Psychologist	Yes	No

5) Social worker or sociologist	Yes	No
6) Vocational counsellor or trainer	Yes	No
7) Ex-addict counsellor	Yes	No
8) Nurse	Yes	No
9) Clergy or religious leader	Yes	No
10) Agency counsellor	Yes	No
11) Other counsellor: specify _____	Yes	No

General Assessment by Therapist

8. Social Functioning (within treatment setting)

1) Well-adjusted socially	Yes	No
2) Co-operative with staff	Yes	No
3) Conforms to treatment regulations	Yes	No
4) Disrupts therapeutic milieu	Yes	No
5) Requires excessive therapeutic attention	Yes	No
6) Physically violent or threatening	Yes	No
7) Other problems: specify_____	Yes	No

9. Diagnosis of medical problems requiring treatment.

10. Source(s) of information for completing report.

1) Personal interview with client	Yes	No
2) Staff members involved in treatment	Yes	No
3) Medical records	Yes	No
4) Client's family	Yes	No
5) Friends of client	Yes	No
6) Other; specify_____	Yes	No

11. Where was tthe questionnaire completed:

 1) At home
 2) At clinic in interview
 3) At clinic by client alone

12. If questionnaire done by client alone was it later reviewed in a client/therapist session?

 Yes _____ No _____

TABLE 6.5
Example of a Summary Assessment
Jones, Mr. Fred
Date of Birth: March 7, 1946

Personal Data:
Fred is an unmarried 30 year old male who works for Canada Post. Fred presented in July 9, 1977 for treatment of alcohol abuse. At the time of presenting, Fred was drinking over ten 12 oz. bottles of 5% beer daily. This pattern had existed for eight months.

Personal History:
Fred is the sixth of seven children. He was born in Smalltown, B.C.

His attitude towards his parents and siblings appears generally positive. He reports however, that as a child he found it difficult to approach his father and that communication with him was infrequent. More recently Fred's relationship with his father, now 73, seems to have improved and he and his father are communicating more freely.

His father continues to work in the fishing industry in Middletown, B.C. although he will likely retire this year. His mother, 65, is a housewife. While his mother rarely, if ever, drinks, it appears that his father has abused alcohol at times.

Fred reports close relationships with his sisters, Helen and Diane, but infrequent association with his older siblings. Diane, a nurse, has been highly instrumental in Fred's involvement in the clinic.

Fred attended a year of study at University in Science, completed a one year course in accounting, and two years in computer programming. He worked as a computer clerk at University but left after ten months due to boredom. Since then he has travelled in Europe, driven taxis, and for nearly three years worked for Canada Post. It seems clear, from Fred's report, that none of these educational or vocational experiences have begun to satisfy his personal needs leading to actualization. He has, in the past, indicated interest in art related vocations but had been dissuaded by guidance counsellors, parents, etc.

Fred appears to have had no encounters with the courts or police other than two charges for drunken driving, and has lived a fairly normal middle class existence. He has interests in some sports (i.e., billiards, baseball), reading, popular music, and movies.

Fred has a sincere desire to realize his treatment goal of abstinence from alcohol. He wishes to attend to healthier aspects of his life (i.e., vocation, sexual relationships, personal satisfaction in social relationships).

Behavioral Assessment
Problems: 1) abuse of alcohol
2) sexual dysfunction—premature ejaculation, impotence
3) vocational dissatisfaction
4) skill deficit in expression of positive and confrontive statements to peers; anxiety in presence of strangers and in crowds.

Etiological Description

1) Fred's immediate concern is his excessive use of alcohol. He first drank alcohol at age 14 but did not regard alcohol as a problem until about three years ago. Beginning three years ago he began to binge drink on the weekends; soon thereafter he started to drink prior to work as well as after. He currently takes alcoholic beverages to work in his thermos. He also spends his lunch break at a nearby hotel where he consumes 2-3 drinks, nearly always beer. He has had only one period of abstinence in the past three years—one week 1½ years ago when he was confined to his home with a broken wrist suffered in a fall when inebriated.

His beverage of choice is beer, which accounts for 90% of his alcohol intake; the remainder is divided about equally between vodka and rum. 75% of his drinking is solitary at home, 10% with heavy drinking acquaintances from the Post Office, and 15% in hotels where he drinks alone for the most part.

Although Fred appears to have used alcohol socially until three years ago, (1 dozen cans of beer per week on average), his consumption increased greatly following the dissolution of an engagement to be married. He and his fiancee Louise had known each other for six months and had several attempts at sexual intercourse, all of which were dissatisfactory for both parties (see below). The engagement was broken following an argument arising out of their mutual sexual frustration. Aside from 1-2 "joints" of marijuana, Fred used no other drugs. He has had no suicide attempts, no psychiatric treatment, nor any treatment for his alcohol abuse.

2) Fred is also very much concerned with his sexual dysfunction. In a limited number of attempts at sexual intercourse with females, he has either ejaculated prior to entry or immediately upon entry. This factor, above all, appears to be highly related to Fred's abuse of alcohol and it is anticipated that successful outcome in this area of his life will greatly contribute to successful outcome in other areas of his life.

In terms of learning theory, it is not difficult to account for Fred's current sexual difficulty. His initial attempt at sexual intercourse occurred at age 20 with a prostitute in Mexico. The experience occurred at a time when he was fatigued from travelling all day and when he was feeling highly anxious about performing the sex act successfully. The attempt was dissatisfactory as Fred ejaculated prematurely. A second experience a week later with another prostitute was terminated by Fred since he was highly anxious and threatened by the prospect of not succeeding a second time. Subsequent experiences with females in Canada have always been overshadowed by fear of sexual failure as in the past. It is important to note also that Fred was under the influence of alcohol which, alone, may be expected to reduce the likelihood of adequate sexual performance.

Fred appears genuinely interested in establishing social and sexual relationships with females but has not dated for over one year. He has not attempted sexual relations since his break-up with Louise.

Fred's masturbatory behavior also appears counterproductive to sustained sexual performance. He indicates he masturbates about twice weekly in a rather hurried fashion so as to complete the act as quickly as possible. Imagery occuring during masturbation occasionally appears to concern his performing successfully with females.

3) Fred completed a two year course in computer programming at the Institute

of Technology and has worked as a computer clerk at the university, as a taxi driver, and as a mailman for Canada Post. He enjoyed little satisfaction either in his course work at the Institute or in the jobs he has held since that time.

Fred has indicated, in the past, interest in art related vocations but he's been dissuaded by guidance counsellors, his parents, etc. He appears positively disposed to holding a job and intends to maintain his job at Canada Post until such time as he determines to return to school or take a different job elsewhere.

As a child Fred was advanced twice to a higher grade suggesting a high level of intellectual ability. I suspect that Fred finds his current position dissatisfactory because it doesn't make sufficient use of his intellect. In addition of course, his job as a mail sorter suggests vocational interests quite divergent from those that Fred has expressed he has.

4) Fred indicated that while his home life as a child was generally satisfactory little communication, if any, existed. He believes that his father was only interested in seeing him established in a career that afforded a sizeable income. Other communications apparently were regarded as bearing little utility.

Fred has indicated feeling ill at ease with people for most of his life. As a child he was physically smaller than his classmates and as such was not invited to participate in competitive sports; in adolescence he felt that his size frustrated his attempts at asking out girls that he was interested in.

More currently, Fred has expressed skill deficit and anxiety in speaking with strangers and in expressing himself in crowds. Furthermore he is often unsure of what to say, either positively or negatively, to people that he doesn't know. It also appears that Fred is unassertive in various social situations.

Techniques of Treatment

1) The following program will be adopted to promote Fred's abstinence from alcohol:
   a) contingency contract will be executed as drafted
   b) covert sensitization of alcohol consumption, covert reinforcement for coping without alcohol
   c) random alcohol monitoring provides external validation for Fred's self-report of abstinence
2) Sexual dysfunction will be dealt with as outlined by Shelton and Ackerman (X), Chapter 9.
3) Fred has already began to deal with his work dissatisfaction. He is completing a battery of vocational and aptitude tests at Canada Manpower. Follow-up of the results will be undertaken as indicated (i.e., enrollment in coursework, change of job)
4) Fred's current skill deficit in interpersonal relationships will be modified through assertive training.

_____   _____
Date of Report   Worker Name

TABLE 6.6
Procedure for Alcohol Monitoring
by Volunteer Monitors

1. Clients requiring alcohol monitoring will be determined each week by staff and listed in the Alcohol Monitoring Book. Volunteer monitors (VM) pick up the briefcase containing The Alcohol Monitoring Book and the alcohol Countermeasures machine from the clinic by 5:00 p.m. Review the list of clients with the staff to assure that each client is available for monitoring that particular evening. Be sure to check the "special considerations" sheet in the monitoring book as well.

2. VM phones each client and determines that the client is receptive to being monitored. (Refusal to provide monitoring sample for any reason is noted under "Comments" on monitoring form without comment to the client; VM judgments on clients' refusal to make themselves available for monitoring are to be avoided.)

Clients *may choose* where they are to be monitored. Most clients will likely remain at home to be monitored. Others, for a variety of reasons, will wish to meet the monitor at the clinic or at an agreed upon location. Determine the time and place where you will monitor each client.

Also, when speaking with the client on the phone remind the client to not smoke and to not use any substances that may confound the analysis (i.e., mouthwashes) until the monitoring is completed.

3. VM makes the rounds by car of listed clients observing the following:

   (a) presenting himself as VM from the clinic;
   (b) determining that the client has not smoked or had any confounding substances in his mouth in the previous 15 minutes and requesting that the client rinse his mouth with water prior to blowing into the alcohol countermeasures machine;
   (c) if the client refuses to present a breath sample when the VM arrives, the VM notes the same in "Comments" section of monitoring form without comment to the client;
   (d) the client is asked for his/her accounting of alcohol intake in previous 12 hours; this information is noted on the monitoring form *without comment to the client* (even if you doubt the validity of the client's self-report).
   (e) the client blows firmly into alcohol countermeasures machine in the manner outlined on the machine; the VM records outcome as PASS, WARN or FAIL on monitoring form without comment to the client. The client is generally allowed only one opportunity to blow into the machine; if the client insists strongly on a second opportunity, allow him to do so about 3 minutes later, noting the situation under "Comments" and describing the second outcome;
   (f) after seeing all clients on the list the VM returns the machine and the monitoring form to the clinic or staff member by 9:00 A.M. the next morning; the VM charges mileage put on his car to the clinic.

Alcohol Monitoring Results

Date _____   Volunteer Monitor _____   Mileage Start _____

Staff Member _____   Mileage Finish _____

Client Name	Monitored: Yes/No (if no, explain)	Time Monitored	Place	Client Self-Report of Alcohol Consumed in Previous 12 Hours	Outcome on Machine (Pass, Warn, Fail)	Comments

Chapter 7

RESEARCH AND EVALUATION

EPILOGUE

THIS SECTION is concerned with one of the more practical, i.e., directly applied, aspects of alcoholism research: treatment effectiveness.

When and how should you determine if your treatment is effective: the last day of treatment? six months later? two years later? through estimates of "improvement" by the client himself? by significant others?

Recent writers [1, 2, 3] have criticized the current status of treatment outcome evaluation. Many studies utilize nonoperationally defined estimates of "improvement" of the client's use of alcohol. Most rely on unsubstantiated client self-reports or the reports of significant others over the phone or by mail, and frequently the individuals who conducted treatment also conduct the evaluation. The weaknesses of such procedures and measures render the reported results of many studies doubtful. The most troubling aspect of the current state of treatment outcome evaluation, however, is the nonuniformity of the evaluation methodologies utilized and the consequent difficulty in comparing the outcomes of different studies.

The object of alcohol treatment outcome evaluation is to determine *"what treatment, by whom, is the most effective for this individual . . . and under which set of circumstances"* [4]. A parallel question concerning outcome evaluation is *who* is to gather *what* information *when* and *how*? These four outcome evaluation issues shall be addressed in order.

Who is to provide the outcome data? There are three major sources of data: the client, the therapist, or some third party which would include members of the client's family, peers, or a neutral observer. All three sources can, in principle, supply either behavioral data or personality data.

The client's data are influenced by: (a) whether he can report his behavior or feelings accurately; (b) his idiosyncratic verbal habits; (c) his desire to please or displease the worker; and (d) his tendency to justify first, his need for treatment, and later, the appropriateness of his termination. Put another way, the client's behavior is sensitive to the demand characteristics of the situation. Such demand characteristics can affect *any* measure where the client knows he is being observed with respect to his progress during or following treatment.

The therapist is biased by: (a) his theories and assumptions concerning alcohol abuse: (b) his involvement with the client and with the client's therapy; and (c) a limited sample of client behaviors—the several hours of verbal report he obtains each week during or following treatment.

Furthermore, both client and therapist measures can be said to suffer from reactivity, whereby the measurement process itself produces unintended sources of influence on the data. The client's knowledge that he is being monitored and that change is expected may affect his performance. The more global or inferential the measure used, the greater the opportunity for reactivity factors to operate.

Third party data are usually more expensive but more objective than those of client or therapist. Much depends on the information they are given and the responses required of them. Many of the constraints on client self report—such as demand characteristics—will also affect the third party measures. Nonetheless, third party measures are much preferred in outcome research because of their relative freedom from the distortions of client and therapist reports, and because they can provide information about client behavior in natural settings.

The "what" of outcome criteria depends on the theoretical convictions and interests of the investigator. One recent major issue has been whether to emphasize personality or more overt and behavioral measures. For example, Poley and Mallett [5] contacted 55 clients (41 male and 14 female) who had been treated for alcoholism at the Edmonton Outpatient Clinic of the Alberta Alcoholism and Drug Abuse Commission. These clients where considered as the "success stories" of the clinic, in that counsellors rated them as having shown the most improvement in the course of treatment. Generally, it was found that while individuals reported satisfactory functioning in terms of overt criteria, such as socioeconomic standards, relations with the community at large, family life and physical health, standard personality tests revealed a residual pattern of anxiety-depression for both men and women which, presumably, would still require treatment.

With its emphasis on changing overt behavior and its rejection of personality change as the primary goal of therapy, the behavioral approach leads to different ways of assessing outcome. Overt behavior has been used effectively as an outcome measure in numerous studies of alcoholic inpatients and outpatients. These studies generally support the effectiveness of behavior modification therapies and encourage more extensive use of behavioral criteria. It is also true that follow-up measures are usually behavioral, and behavioral indices may be expected to correlate more highly with behavioral measures than personality measures.

If alcohol consumption is used rather than personality tests as an outcome measure, should it serve as the *sole* criterion of outcome? While abstinence has been used as the only criterion of treatment outcome in many reports in the past, it has recently become the subject of considerable criticism. Such a unidimensional view of treatment outcome leaves aside other important life variables. That abstinence is not fundamental to improvement on other dimensions and that it may, in fact, be *negatively* related to general improvement has been reported in the literature [2, 3, 6, 7]. Moreover, life space variables such as occupational status, health, marital status or involvement with the court system are less subject to client misrepresentation than client report of use of alcohol.

Once discharged from treatment, alcohol abusers are notoriously prone to relapse. That treatment outcome can therefore be influenced by the length of the follow-up interval is evident. *Of those who relapse* after treatment, 50% do so by one month, 66% by three months, about 75% by six months and 95% by one year [8]. The same authors note that while consumption patterns at six months are predictive of significant improvement, a follow-up interval of one year would provide additional certainty of client performance.

So far then, we have advocated the collection of multiple outcome data, over the period of one year by a third party. Still, the source of the data gathered represents a potential extra treatment influence on the treatment outcome results. Data reflecting actual client performance may be collected from a variety of sources including informants who are able to observe the client in the community, raters who follow the client into his home or work setting, inferred performance measures or direct observation in the clinic.

Informants

If one is interested in the overt, social behavior of the client, it would seem appropriate to seek data from friends or relatives who have an opportunity to observe the client in natural settings. This method has been used only sporadically with outpatient alcoholic populations. The use of informants requires consideration of certain methodological issues, including sampling bias, opportunity to observe the relevant behavior, and knowledge that the client has been treated for alcohol abuse. Finally, there are the practical problems of securing co-operation from informants who may have little at stake in the outcome of the therapy.

Direct Observation

The observation of problem behaviors in natural settings has been championed by behavioral practitioners, though it is most commonly done with children, in homes or in schools, or with hospitalized patients. The performance of alcoholic clients may also be assessed through random alcohol monitoring. These observational procedures have their own methodological problems. These problems include the question of machine reliability, generalizability of observational data, reliability of data sampling, and the problem of the effect of the observer upon the interaction which he observes. Observational data are expensive to collect, but their demonstrated utility in the assessment of change in drinking patterns makes the effort worthwhile for outcome evaluation purposes.

Client Records

Client behavior in natural settings may be inferred from records such as school and work records, number of arrests, and number of hospitalizations. Such measures are inherently meaningful. If they reflect positive results they provide strong evidence of treatment effectiveness. Negative results, however, are more difficult to interpret. The vulnerability of these public record measures to situational factors outside the treatment context—e.g. illness, fluctuations in employment opportunities—are such that they may fail to reflect a moderate but true treatment effect.

In sum, many researchers involved in treatment outcome evaluation report dissatisfaction with global measures of change and data produced by either the client and/or the worker. There is a movement away from the single criterion of abstinence towards the use of *multiple outcome criteria based on the client's presenting complaints.* Data gathered in the natural environment by third parties over a follow-up interval of one year, while expensive, is advocated. Random monitoring of alcohol use and data relative to the client's educational and work situation, progress in related treatment goals, interpersonal relationships, marital status, hospitalization and incarceration, all help reflect outcome concerns of treatment programs that are broadly based.

For an outstanding example of a study that incorporated many of the points advocated above, refer to reports by Sobell and his colleagues [1, 9]. The reader is also reminded of the broadly based Continuous Data Questionnaire (CDQ), developed by Poley, Vibe, Vibe, Kyle and other staff of the Alternatives Program for Alcohol and Drug Dependencies in Vancouver, and described in the preceding chapter. The CDQ provides a means of monitoring reported change on primary life-space criteria throughout the assessment, treatment and follow-up process. Goal attainment scaling [10, 11] also offers the worker a set of procedures for scaling treatment goals and assessing the extent to which they have been attained.

An excellent study of treatment outcome evaluation is the Rand Report [12] which reports on data collected on nearly 30,000 clients who had entered treatment in 44 comprehensive treatment centers throughout the United States. It indicates that clients of these centers show substantial improvement in drinking behaviour after treatment, both at 6 months and 18 months following intake. The rate of improvement is *70 per cent for several different outcome indicators.* Although this improvement rate is impressive, the report stresses that the improved clients include only a relatively small number who are longterm abstainers. The majority of 'improved clients' are either drinking moderate amounts of alcohol—at levels below what would be considered alcoholic drinking—or engaging in alternating periods of drinking and abstention.

Another major finding of the study was that among clients with formal treatment there were no major differences in remission rates among different treatment settings, such as hospitalization, halfway houses, or outpatient care; nor were there differences among the different types of therapeutic techniques, such as group therapy, individual therapy, or Antabuse treatment. It appears that the administration of treatment is more important than the actual type of treatment itself. Moreover, there is the fact that different types of treatment are applicable to different types of clients. Overall, the report provides a comprehensive and scientific evaluation of the effectiveness of many alcoholism treatment centers in the United States.

This chapter has presented a number of the difficulties involved in evaluating alcoholism programs. Researchers in fact tend to be rather cautious in their statements about the effectiveness of treatment since they are highly aware of the methodological problems in design and measurement. For the practicing clinician or client in treatment, however, a more definite answer to the question 'How effective is treatment?' is required. In the preceding chapters (Chapters 4−6) some statistics have been presented along with treatment methods. The authors could therefore offer the following statement as a summary of overall effectiveness for general treatment efforts and a target for future programs. After a year of treatment we would expect 40% of the clients in a typical program to be successfully treated or well on their way toward successful treatment. Moreover, 70% of the clients in the program would show at least noticeable improvement. Thus there is every reason to be hopeful of a positive outcome at the same time that we strive to improve our efforts on behalf of our alcohol-dependent clients.

APPENDIXES

Appendix A

HOW TO GET HELP

Individuals desiring to modify their use of alcohol can seek help from a variety of therapeutic agents. The following are recommended as primary considerations:

1. *Behavioral treatment programs:* A number of "broad-spectrum" behavioral programs for the treatment of alcohol abuse have been established in the past decade. No central registry of such programs exist. Nonetheless, most behavioral treatment programs have liaison with the psychology departments of nearby universities. Department faculty members would likely be able to direct interested individuals to the programs they want. Most behavioral programs are prepared to assist their clients to attain control over their use of alcohol as well as to abstain from alcohol altogether.

2. *Drinkwatchers:* Although a relatively new organization, Drinkwatchers may be found in many major North American cities. Drinkwatchers offers each member group support for his or her choice of drinking goals whether it be controlled drinking or abstinence. More on Drinkwatchers groups in North America can be obtained from Drinkwatchers, P.O. Box 179, Haverstraw, New York, 10927.

3. *Alcoholics Anonymous:* Alcoholics Anonymous (A.A.) is most appropriate for the individual who is convinced he would be better off not drinking at all and would like support for such a decision. A.A. has helped many people around the world and it is always available to speak with those for whom alcohol has become a problem. Alcoholics Anonymous may be found in virtually every community of any size. Information is also available from: Alcoholics Anonymous General Service Office, P.O. Box 459, Grand Central Station, New York, 10017.

4. *Other Sources:* Each community has mental health agencies that can direct interested individuals to alcohol treatment facilities. Crisis lines, major hospitals, social workers, medical doctors and ministers can generally be counted on to have some information describing treatment facilities in the local community. Listings of treatment centres may also be found under the category of "Alcoholism Treatment" or some similar heading in the Yellow Pages of city telephone directories.

Appendix B

WHERE TO FIND INFORMATION

Classified Abstract Archive of the Alcohol Literature (CAAAL). Represents approximately 10,000 abstracts of the literature on alcohol studies. Developed and kept up to date by the Rutgers Center of Alcohol Studies, Rutgers University, New Brunswick, N.J. CAAAL may be maintained by other special libraries in the field.

Quarterly Journal of Studies on Alcohol. The major international journal in the field of alcohol studies. Published by the Rutgers Center of Alcohol Studies, Rutgers University, New Brunswick, N.J.

Directory of Special Libraries and Information Centers. Edited by M. L. Young, H. C. Young and A. T. Kruzas. Gale Research Company, Detroit, Michigan, 48226. Includes listing of special libraries in the field of alcohol studies.

Institute for Scientific Information, 325 Chestnut Street, Philadelphia, Pa. 19106. Uses key words to obtain references relevant to a specific topic, from computer storage of titles, abstracts, authors in various fields, including alcohol research. Result is to provide a "current awareness service" to keep individuals up to date with literature in their field.

National Clearinghouse for Alcohol Information, National Institute on Alcohol Abuse and Alcoholism. U.S. Dep't. of Health, Education and Welfare, P. O. Box 2345, Rockville, Maryland. Provides abstracts of alcohol literature in various categories on a monthly and quarterly basis.

A Dictionary of Words about Alcohol by M. Keller, Rutgers University, New Brunswick, N.J.

Catalog of Publications. National Council on Alcoholism, Inc., 2 Park Avenue, New York, N.Y., 10016.

Labyrinth. A current awareness service on alcohol and drug abuse published weekly under the sponsorship of the Non-Medical Use of Drugs Directorate by Orba Information Ltd., 265 Craig Street West, Montreal, Quebec, H2Z 1H6.

Agency Catalogue. Published by the Non-Medical Use of Drugs Directorate, Department of National Health and Welfare, Ottawa.

Alcoholism Treatment Facilities Directory (U.S. and Canada). Published by Alcohol and Drug Problems Association of North America, 1130 Seventeenth Street N.W., Washington, D.C., 20036.

Grassroots Directory of Drug Information and Treatment Organizations. Published by National Co-ordinating Council on Drug Education Inc., Suite 212, Connecticut Avenue N.W., Washington, D.C. 20036.

International Council on Alcohol and Alcoholism, Case Postale 140, 1001 Lausanne, Switzerland.

The Institute for the Study of Drug Dependence. Chandos House, 2 Queen Anne Street, London, WIM OBR.
Directory of Training Facilities for the Helping Professions in Canada by Glen Kunzman. Counselling Service, 474 University Center, University of Manitoba, Winnipeg, Manitoba.

Addictions. A booklet published quarterly by the Addiction Research Foundation of Ontario, 33 Russell Street, Toronto M5S 2SI. Contents include a variety of articles selected on the basis of their potential interest to people engaged in research, treatment, or education in the field of alcoholism or other drug research.
Addictive Behaviours. Published by Pergamon Press Ltd., Headington Hill Hall, Oxford OX3 OBW. Includes relevant research in the area of addictions: obesity, smoking, alcohol and drug use.
Alcoholism: Clinical and Experimental Research. Published by Grune & Stratton, Inc. 111 Fifth Avenue, New York, N.Y. 10003. The official journal of the American Medical Society on Alcoholism and The Research Society on Alcoholism; contains recent articles, book reviews, recent books, future meetings, news from the above societies, and papers presented at seminars and conferences.
The American Journal of Drug and Alcohol Abuse. Published by Marcel Dekker Journals, P. 0. Box 11305, Church Street Station, New York, N.Y. 10249. Presents a medically oriented forum for the exchange of ideas between preclinical, clinical, and social modalities involved in the study and treatment of drug abuse and alcoholism.
International Journal of the Addictions. Published by Marcel Dekker Journals, P. O. Box 11305, Church Street Station, New York, New York 10249. Published eight times annually as a medium for worldwide communication among laymen and professionals in research, training, and treatment in the field of addictions.
The Journal. Published by the Addiction Research Foundation, 33 Russell Street, Toronto, Canada M5S 2SI. A monthly newsletter containing contemporary and international findings in the drug abuse and alcoholism field. Lists new books, projections, as well as coming conferences, seminars and training programs.

National Council on Alcoholism, Inc. 733 Third Ave., New York, New York 10017.
Addiction Research Foundation, 33 Russell St., Toronto, Ontario.
Promotion and Prevention Directorate, 102 Bloor Street West, Suite 1004, Toronto, Ontario M5S IM8.

REFERENCES

REFERENCES

CHAPTER 1

1. Irwin, S. *Drugs of Abuse. An Introduction to their Actions and Potential Hazards.* Beloit, Wisconsin: Student Association for the Study of Hallucinogens, 1970.

2. *Final Report of the Commission of Inquiry into the Non-Medical Use of Drugs.* Gerald LeDain, Chairman, Ottawa: Queen's Printer, 1973.

3. Archibald, H.D. Changing drinking patterns in Ontario—some Implications. *Addictions,* **20,** 2-17, 1973.

4. Merton, R.K. *Social Theory and Social Structure.* New York: Free Press, 1957.

5. Lutz, H.F. *Viticulture and Brewing in the Ancient Orient.* Leipzig: J.C. Heinrichs, 1922.

6. Edwards, G. Epidemiology applied to alcoholism, a review and an examination of purposes. *Quarterly Journal of Studies on Alcohol,* **34,** 28-56, 1973.

7. *First Special Report to the U.S. Congress on Alcohol and Health.* U.S. Department of Health, Education and Welfare, 1971.

8. *Annual Report of the Alcoholism and Drug Addiction Research Foundation of Ontario.* Ontario, 1972.

9. Vibe, G. & Thistle, R. "The effects of sex differences, job satisfaction, and personality variables on drinking behaviour in an employed population." Project supported by the Non-Medical Use of Drugs Directorate, Health & Welfare, Canada, 1978.

10. Ledermann, S. *Alcool, alcoolisme, alcoolisation: Donn's scientifiques de caractere physiologique, economique et social.* (Institute National de'Etudes Demographique Traveux et Documents, Cahier No. 29). Paris: Press Universitaires de France, 1956.

11. Efron, V. Keller, M. & Guriolo, C. *Statistics on consumption of alcohol and on alcoholism.* New Brunswick, New Jersey: Rutgers Center of Alcohol Studies, 1972.

12. Klatskin, G. Alcohol and its relation to liver damage, *Gastroenterology.* **41,** 443-451, 1961.

13. Ranking, J.G., Schmidt, W. & Popham, R.E. Epidemiology of alcoholic liver disease—insights and problems. Paper presented at the Joint Royal College of Physicians and Surgeons of Canada—Canadian Society for Clinical Investigation Symposium: "The Alcoholic and Liver Disease." Jan. 1972.

14. Latchford, M.A. & McDonald, L. *Comparative international study of alcoholism.* Unpublished Research Paper for the Commission of Inquiry into the Non-Medical Use of Drugs, 1971.

15. Seely, J.R. Death by liver cirrhosis and the price of beverage alcohol. *Canadian Medical Association Journal,* **83,** 1361-1366, 1960.

16. Smart, R. & Fejer, D. Drug use among adolescents and their parents: closing the generation gap in mood modification. *Journal of Abnormal Psychology,* **79,** 153-160, 1972.

17. Bacon, M. and Jones, Mary Brush. *Teen-Age Drinking,* New York: Thomas Y. Crowell Co., 1968.

18. Miller, P.M. *Behavioral Treatment of Alcoholism.* New York: Pergammon, 1976.

19. Jellinek, E.M. "Death from alcoholism" in the United States in 1940; a statistical analysis. *Quarterly Journal of Studies on Alcohol,* 1942, **3,** 465-494.

141

20. Liquor for the hungry. *Illinois Church Action on Alcohol Problems News,* Naperville, Illinois, Jan. 1975, No. 1.

21. Cahalan, Don. *Problem Drinkers A National Survey.* San Francisco, Cal: Jossey-Bass, Inc., 1970.

CHAPTER 2

1. Wallgren, H. & Barry, H. *Actions of Alcohol.* Amsterdam: Elsevier Publishing Company, 1970.

2. Jellinek, E.M. *The Disease Concept of Alcoholism.* Connecticut: Hillhouse Press, 1960.

3. Miller, W.R. & Munoz, R.F. *How to Control Your Drinking.* Englewood Cliffs, New Jersey: Prentice-Hall, Inc., 1976, pp. 10-15.

4. *Management of the Alcoholic Patient.* St. Paul's Hospital, Vancouver, B.C., 1975.

5. *First Special Report to the U.S. Congress on Alcohol and Health.* U.S. Department of Health, Education and Welfare, Public Health Service, U.S. Government Printing Office, 1973.

6. Lieber, C.S. "The Metabolism of Alcohol". *Scientific American,* Vol. **234,** No. 3, March 1976.

7. Cohen, S. *Physician's Manual on Alcoholism.* Saskatoon, Saskatchewan: The Western Producer, 1966.

8. Tucker, B. *"Pregnancy and Drugs," Addictions.* Toronto: Addiction Research Foundation of Ontario, 1975.

9. Jones, K.L., Smith, D.W., Vlleland, C.N., & Streisguth, A.P. Pattern of malformation in offspring of chronic alcoholic mothers. *Lancet,* **1,** pp. 1267-1271, 1973.

10. Sandor, S., Snels, D. Action of Ethanol on the Prenatal Development of Albino Rats. *Rev. Roum. Embroyol. Cytol. Sep. Embroyol.* **8:** 105-118, 1971.

11. Tze, W.J., Lee, M. Adverse effects of maternal alcohol consumption on pregnancy and foetal growth in rats. *Nature* **257:** 479-480, 1975.

12. Chernoff, G.F. A mouse model of the fetal alcohol syndrome. *Teratology* **11:**14a, 1975.

13. Brecher, E.M. & the Editors of Consumer Reports, *Licit and Illicit Drugs,* Boston-Toronto: Little, Brown & Co., 1972.

14. *Final Report of the Commission of Inquiry into the Non-Medical Use of Drugs,* Gerald LeDain, Chairman. Ottawa: Queen's Printer for Canada, 1973.

15. Wolfgang, M. & Strohm, R.B. The relationship between alcohol and criminal homicide. *Quarterly Journal of Studies on Alcohol,* **17,** pp. 411-425, 1956.

16. Bowden, K.M., Wilson, D.W. & Turner, L.K. A survey of blood alcohol testing in Victoria (1951 to 1956). *Medical Journal of Australia,* **452,** 13-15, 1958.

CHAPTER 3

1. *Final Report of the Commission of Inquiry into the Non-Medical Use of Drugs.* Gerald LeDain, Chairman. Ottawa: Queen's Printer, 1973.

2. McCord, W., McCord, J. & Gudeman, J. *Origins of Alcoholism.* Stanford, California: Stanford University Press, 1960.

3. Perls, F., Hefferline, R.F., & Goodman, P. *Gestalt Therapy: Excitement and Growth in the Human Personality.* New York: Dell Publishing, 1951.

4. Steiner, C. *Games Alcoholics Play.* New York: Grove Press, 1971.

5. Levitsky, A. & Perls, F. The rules and games of gestalt therapy. In Fagan, J. & Shepherd, I. (Eds.) *Gestalt Therapy Now.* Palo Alto, California: Science and Behavior Books, 1970.

6. Buss, A.R., & Poley, W. *Individual Differences: Traits and Factors.* New York: Gardner Press Inc. 1976.

7. Poley, W. Personality, predisposition, conditionability and alcohol consumption: a psychobiological approach. In R. Nutter & W. Poley (Eds.) *Proceedings of the Sixth Annual Research Symposium of the Alberta Alcoholism and Drug Abuse Commission.* Edmonton: Alberta Alcoholism and Drug Abuse Commission, 1974.

8. Wilsnack, S.C. Femininity by the Bottle. *Addictions,* **20:** 2-19, 1973.

9. May, R. Existential Psychology. In R. May (Ed.) *Existential Psychology.* New York: Random House, 1961, pp. 11-51.

10. Goodwin, D.W., Schulsinger, F., Hermansen, L., Guze, S.B. & Winokur, G. Alcohol problems in adoptees raised apart from alcoholic biological parents. *Archives of General Psychiatry,* **28:** 238-243, 1973.

11. Roe, A. Children of alcoholic parentage raised in foster homes. In *Alcohol, Science and Society,* published by *Quarterly Journal of Studies on Alcohol,* 1974, pp. 115-127.

12. Wallgren, H. & Barry, H. *Actions of Alcohol.* Amsterdam: Elsevier Publishing Company, 1970.

13. Veale, W.L. Neurohumoural correlates of alcohol consumption. In R. Nutter & W. Poley (Eds.) *Proceedings of the Sixth Annual Research Symposium of the Alberta Alcoholism and Drug Abuse Commission.* Edmonton: Alberta Alcoholism and Drug Abuse Commission, 1974.

14. Williams, R.J. Biochemical individuality and cellular nutrition: prime factors in alcoholism. *Quarterly Journal of Studies on Alcohol,* **20:** 452-463, 1959.

CHAPTER 4

1. Emrick, C. "Relative effectiveness of alcohol abuse treatment." Unpublished paper, 1978.

2. Edwards, G. Alcoholism: the analysis of treatment. In R.E. Popham (Ed.) *Alcohol and Alcoholism,* Toronto: University of Toronto Press, 1970.

3. Edwards, G. & Guthrie, S. A comparison of inpatient and outpatient treatment of alcohol dependence. *Lancet,* **1:** 467-468, 1966.

4. Edwards, G. & Guthrie, S. A controlled trial of inpatient and outpatient treatment of alcohol dependency, *Lancet,* **1:** 555-559, 1967.

5. Gallant, D.M. Evaluation of compulsory treatment of the alcoholic municipal court offender. In N.K. Mello and J.H. Mendelsohn (Eds.) *Recent Advances in Studies of Alcoholism: An interdisciplinary symposium, Washington, D.C., June 25-27, 1970.* Rockville, Maryland: National Institute of Alcohol Abuse and Alcoholism, 1971.

6. Wanberg, K., Horn, J., & Fairchild, D. Hospital versus community treatment of alcoholism problems. *International Journal of Mental Health,* **3:** 160-176, 1974.

7. Baekeland, F., Lundwall, L., & Kissin, B. Methods for the treatment of chronic alcoholism: a critical appraisal. In R. Gibbins, Y. Israd, H. Kalant, R. Popham, W. Schmidt, and R. Smart (Eds.) *Research Advances in Alcohol and Drug Problems: Volume Two.* New York: John Wiley & Sons, 1975.

8. Baekeland, F. Evaluation of treatment methods in chronic alcoholism. In B. Kissin and H. Begleiter (Eds.) *Treatment and Rehabilitation of the Chronic Alcoholic.* New York: Plenum Press, 1977.

9. Emrick, C. "Alcoholism treatment." Handout for presentation at the 8th Annual Meeting of the Society for Psychotherapy Research. Madison, Wisconsin, June 23, 1977.

10. Gibbs, L., & Flanagan, J. Prognostic indicators of alcoholism treatment outcome. *The International Journal of the Addictions,* **12:** 1097-1141, 1977.

11. Gerard, D.L., & Saenger, G. *Outpatient Treatment of Alcoholism.* Toronto: University of Toronto Press, 1966.

12. Gallant, D.M., Bishop, M.P., Stoy, B., Faulkner, M.A., & Paternostro, L. The value of a "first contact" group intake session in an alcoholism outpatient clinic: Statistical confirmation. *Psychosomatics,* **7:** 349-352, 1969.

13. Panepinto, W.C., & Higgins, M.J. Keeping alcoholics in treatment: Effective follow-through procedures. *Quarterly Journal of Studies on Alcohol,* **30:** 414-419, 1969.
14. Chafetz, M.E., & Blane, H. T. Alcohol-crisis treatment approach and establishment of treatment relations with alcoholics. *Psychological Reports,* **12:** 862, 1963.
15. Chafetz, M.E., Blane, H.T., Abraham, H.S., Golner, J., Lacy, E., McCourt, W. F., Clark, E., & Meyers, W. Establishing treatment relations with alcoholics. *Journal of Nervous and Mental Diseases,* **134:** 395-409, 1962.
16. Demone, H.W. Experiments in referral to alcoholism clinics. *Quarterly Journal of Studies on Alcohol,* **24:** 485-502, 1963.
17. Koumans, A.J.R., & Muller, J.J. Use of letters to increase motivation for treatment in alcoholics. *Psychological Reports,* **16:** 1152, 1965.
18. Koumans, A.J., Muller, J.J., & Miller, C.F. Use of telephone calls to increase motivation for treatment in alcoholics. *Psychological Reports,* **21:** 347-348, 1967.
19. Malmoe, S., Rosenthal, R., Blane, H.T., Chafetz, M.E., & Wolf, I. The doctor's voice: postdictor of successful referral of alcoholic patients. *Journal of Abnormal Psychology,* **72:** 78-84, 1967.
20. Mayer, J. Initial alcoholism clinic attendance of patients with legal referrals. *Quarterly Journal of Studies on Alcohol,* **33:** 814-816, 1972.
21. Knox, W.J. Attitudes of psychiatrists and psychologists toward alcoholism. *American Journal of Psychiatry,* **127:** 1675-1679, 1971.
22. Victor, M. & Wolfe, S.M. Causation and treatment of the alcohol withdrawal syndrome. In P.G. Bourne & R. Fox (Eds.) *Alcoholism: Progress in Research and Treatment,* New York: Academic Press, 1973.
23. Victor, M. Treatment of alcohol intoxication and the withdrawal syndrome. In Peter Bourne (Ed.) *A Treatment Manual for Acute Drug Abuse Emergencies.* Rockville, Maryland: National Institute on Drug Abuse, 1975.
24. Knott, D.H., & Beard, J.D. Diagnosis and the therapy of acute withdrawal from alcohol. In Peter Bourne (Ed.) *A Treatment Manual for Acute Drug Abuse Emergencies.* Rockville, Maryland: National Institute on Drug Abuse, 1975.
25. Alcoholics Anonymous, *The Fellowship of Alcoholics.* New York: 1976.
26. Trice, H.M. & Roman, P.M. "Sociopsychological predictors of affiliation with Alcoholics Anonymous: A longitudinal study of "treatment success". *Social Psychiatry,* **5:** 51-59, 1970.
27. Forrest, G.G. *The Diagnosis and Treatment of Alcoholism.* Springfield, Ill.: Charles C. Thomas, 1973.
28. Gelman, G.I.P. *The Sober Alcoholic: An Organizational Analysis of Alcoholics Anonymous.* New Haven, Conn.: College and University Press, 1964.
29. Alcoholics Anonymous. *Profile of an AA Meeting.* New York: Alcoholics Anonymous World Services, Inc., 1972.
30. C., Bill. The growth and effectiveness of Alcoholics Anonymous in a Southwestern city. *Quarterly Journal of Studies on Alcohol,* **26:** 279-284, 1965.
31. Ditman, K.S. A controlled experiment on the use of court probation for drunk arrests *American Journal of Psychiatry,* **124:** 160-163, 1967.
32. Wilson W. *Alcoholics anonymous: the story of how many thousands of men and women have recovered from alcoholism* (3rd edition). New York: A.A. World Services, 1976.
33. Leach, B., & Norris, J. The development of Alcoholics Anonymous. In B. Kissin and H. Begleiter (Eds.) *The Biology of Alcoholism: Volume 5.* New York: Plenum Press, 1977.
34. Winters, Ariel. *The Purpose of DW.* Drinkwatchers Newsletter, December, 1976.
35. Adams, J. *Drink to Your Health.* New York: Harper's Magazine Press, 1976.
36. McNamee, H.B., Mello, N.K., & Mendelson, J.H. Experimental analysis of drinking patterns of alcoholics: Concurrent psychiatric observations. *American Journal of Psychiatry* **124:** 1063-1069, 1968.
37. Engle, K.B., & Williams, T.K. Effects on an ounce of vodka on alcoholics' desire for alcohol. *Quarterly Journal of Studies on Alcohol,* **33:** 1099-1105, 1972.

38. Marlatt, G.A., Demming, B., & Reid, J.B. Loss of control drinking in alcoholics: An experimental analogue. *Journal of Abnormal Psychology*, 81: 233-241, 1973.
39. Bolman, W.M. Abstinence versus permissiveness in the psychotherapy of alcoholism *Archives of General Psychiatry*, 12: 456-463, 1965.
40. Pattison, E.M. A critique of abstinence criteria in the treatment of alcoholism *International Journal of Social Psychiatry*, 14: 268-276, 1968.
41. Lovibond, S.H., & Caddy, G. Discriminated aversive control in the moderation of alcoholics' drinking behavior.*Behavior Therapy*, 1: 437-444, 1970.
42. Caddy, G.R., & Lovibond, S.H. Self-regulation and discriminated aversive conditioning in the modification of alcoholics' drinking behavior. *Behavior Therapy*, 7: 223-230, 1976.
43. Vogel-Sprott, M. Self-evaluation of performance and the ability to discriminate blood alcohol concentrations. *Journal of Studies on Alcohol*, 36: 1-10, 1975.
44. Huber, H., Karlin, R., & Nathan, P.E. Blood alcohol level discrimination by nonalcoholics: The role of internal and external cues. *Journal of Studies on Alcohol*, 37: 27-39, 1976.
45. Cohen, M., Liebson, I., & Faillace, L. A technique for establishing controlled drinking in chronic alcoholics. *Diseases of the Nervous System*, 33: 46-49, 1972.
46. Cohen, M., Liebson, I., & Faillace, L. Controlled drinking by chronic alcoholics over extended periods of free access. *Psychological Reports*, 32: 1107-1110, 1973.
47. Cohen, M., Liebson, I.A., Faillace, L.A. & Allen, R.P. Moderate drinking by chronic alcoholics. *Journal of Nervous and Mental Diseases*, 153: 434-444, 1971.
48. Cohen, M., Liebson, I.A., Faillace, L.A., & Spears, W. Alcoholicm: Controlled drinking and incentives for abstinence. *Psychological Reports*, 28: 575-580, 1971.
49. Bigelow, G., Liebson, I., & Griffiths, R. Alcoholic drinking: Suppression by a brief time-out procedure. *Behavior Research and Therapy*, 12: 107-115, 1974.
50. Mills, K.C., Sobell, M.B., & Schaefer, H.H. Training social drinking as an alternative to abstinence for alcoholics. *Behavior Therapy*, 2: 18-27, 1971.
51. Sobell, M.B. & Sobell, L.C. Individualized behavior therapy for alcoholics. *Behavior Therapy*, 4: 49-72, 1973.
52. Sobell, M.B. & Sobell, L.C. A brief technical report on the MOBAT: an inexpensive portable test for determining blood alcohol concentration. *Journal of Applied Behavior Analysis*, 8: 117-120, 1975.
53. Sobell, M.B. & Sobell, L.C. Second year treatment outcome of alcoholics treated by individualized behavior therapy: Results. *Behavior Research and Therapy* 14: 195-215, 1976.
54. Hamburg, S. Behavior therapy in alcoholism: A critical review of broad-spectrum approaches. *Journal of Studies on Alcohol*, 36: 69-87, 1975.
55. Miller, P.M. *Behavioral Treatment of Alcoholism*. New York: Pergamon, 1976.
56. Nathan, P.E. Alcoholism. In H. Leitenberg, (Ed.) *Handbook of Behavior modification* Englewood Cliffs, New Jersey: Prentice-Hall, 1976.
57. Lloyd, R.W., Jr., & Salzberg, H.C. Controlled social drinking: An alternative to abstinence as a treatment goal for some alcohol abusers. *Psychological Bulletin*, 82: 815-842, 1975.
58. Miller, W.R., & Munoz, R.F. *How to control your drinking* Englewood Cliffs, New Jersey: Prentice-Hall, 1976.
59. *Occupational Alcoholism: Some Problems and Some Solutions*, National Institute on Alcohol Abuse and Alcoholism, U.S. Dept., of Health, Education, and Welfare, 1975, pp. 3-14.
60. Patton, Earl M. When the employee will accept treatment and rehabilitation. *Probe Conference*, 1972, Vancouver: Workmen's Compensation Board of British Columbia.
61. Zentner, A. Alcoholism and the job. *International Psychiatry Clinics, Occupational Psychiatry*, Vol. 6, No. 4, 1969, pp. 277-286.
62. *Employee Assistance Programs*, Addiction Research Foundation of Ontario, Toronto, Ontario.
63. Burgess, L.B. *Alcohol and Your Health*, Charles Publishing Company Inc., 1973, p. 70.

64. Straus, Robert, & Bacon, Sheldon D., Alcoholism and social stability: A study of occupational integration of 2,023 male clinic patients. *Quarterly Journal of Studies in Alcohol,* **12:** 231-260, 1951.
65. Trice, H.M. & Roman, P.M. *Spirits and Demons at Work: Alcohol and Other Drugs on the Job,* New York State School of Industrial and Labour Relations. Ithaca, New York: Cornell University Press, 1972, pp. 101-103.
66. Lisansky, E.S. *The Woman Alcoholic Ann. Amer. Acad. Polit. Soc. Sci.* **315:** 73-81, 1958.
67. Curlee, J. A Comparison of male and female patients at an alcoholism treatment centre. *Journal of Psychology,* **74:** 239-247, 1970.
68. Lindbeck, V.L. The Woman Alcoholic: A Review of the Literature. *The International Journal of the Addictions,* **7:** 567-580, 1972.
69. Schuckit, M. The Alcoholic Woman: A literature review. *Psychiatry in Medicine* **3** (1): 37-43, 1972.
70. Gomberg, S. Women and Alcoholism. In *Women in Therapy* ed. by Violet Franks Vasanti Burtle. New York: Brunner/Mazel, 1974, 169-190.
71. Pinder, L. Boyle, B. Double Jeopardy Employees. *Addictions,* Fall, 1977.
72. McLachlan, J.F. Research Note No. 7. *Donwood Institute,* Toronto, Ont. 1977.

CHAPTER 5

1. Lubetkin, B.S., Ribers, P.C. & Rosenberg, C.M. Difficulties of disulfiram therapy with alcoholics *Quarterly Journal of Studies on Alcohol,* **32:** 168-171, 1971.
2. Baekeland, J., Lundwall, L., Kissin, B., & Shanahan, T. Correlates of outcome in disulfiram treatment of alcoholism. *Journal of Nervous and Mental Diseases,* **153:** 1-9, 1971.
3. Lundwall, L., & Baekeland, F. Disulfiram treatment of alcoholism; a review. *Journal of Nervous and Mental Diseases,* **153:** 381-394, 1971.
4. Ditman, K.S. Review and evaluation of current drug therapies in alcoholism *Psychosomatic Medicine,* **28:** 667-677, 1966.
5. Mottin, J.L. Drug-induced attenuation of alcohol consumption. *Quarterly Journal of Studies on Alcohol,* **34:** 444-472, 1973.
6. Viamontes, J.A. Review of drug effectiveness in the treatment of alcoholism. *American Journal of Psychiatry,* **128:** 1570-1571, 1972.
7. Abuzzahab, F.S., & Anderson, F.J. A review of L.S.D. treatment in alcoholism *International Pharmacopsychiatry,* **6:** 223-235, 1971.
8. Bowen, W.T., Soskin, R.A., & Chotlos, J.W. Lysergic acid diethylamide as a variable in the hospital treatment of alcoholism; a follow-up study. *Journal of Nervous and Mental Diseases,* **150:** 111-118, 1970.
9. Johnson, F.G. LSD in the treatment of alcoholism. *American Journal of Psychiatry,* **126:** 481-487, 1969.
10. Tomsovic, M., & Edwards, R.V. Lysergide treatment of schizophrenic and nonschizophrenic alcoholics: a controlled evaluation. *Quarterly Journal of Studies on Alcohol,* **31:** 932-949, 1970.
11. Birk, S. (Ed.) *Biofeedback: Behavioral Medicine.,* New York: Grune & Stratton, 1973.
12. Steffen, J.J. Electromyographically induced relaxation in the treatment of chronic alcohol abuse. *Journal of Consulting and Clinical Psychology,* **43:** 275, 1975.
13. Forrest, G.G. *The Diagnosis and Treatment of Alcoholism.* Springfield, Ill.: Charles C. Thomas, 1973.
14. Bratter, T.E. Reality Therapy: a group psychotherapeutic approach with adolescent alcoholics. *Annals of the New York Academy of Sciences,* **233:** 104-114, 1974.
15. Stein, A., & Friedman, E. Group therapy with alcoholics In H.I. Kaplan and B.J. Sadock (Eds.) *Comprehensive Group Psychotherapy.* Baltimore: Williams & Wilkins, 1971.
16. Steiner, Claude *Games Alcoholics Play.* New York: Grove Press, 1971.

17. Baekeland, F., Lundwall, L., & Kissin, B. Methods for the treatment of chronic alcoholism: a critical appraisal. In R. Gibbins, Y. Israd, H. Kalant, R. Popham, W. Schimdt, and R. Smart (Eds.) *Research Advances in Alcohol and Drug Problems: Volume Two.* New York: John Wiley & Sons, 1975.

18. Westfield, D.R. Two years' experience of group methods in the treatment of male alcoholics in a Scottish mental hospital. *British Journal of Addictions,* **67**: 267-276, 1972.

19. Pokorny, A.D., Miller, B.A., Kanas, T., & Balles, J. Effectiveness of extended aftercare in the treatment of alcoholism. *Quarterly Journal of Studies on Alcohol,* **34**: 435-443, 1973.

20. Wolff, K., Hospitalized alcoholic patients. III. Motivating alcoholics through group psychotherapy. *Hospital and Community Psychiatry,* **19**: 206-209, 1968.

21. Kish, G.B., & Hermann, H.T. The Fort Meade alcoholism treatment program: a follow-up study. *Quarterly Journal of Studies on Alcohol,* **32**: 628-635, 1971.

22. Tomsovic, M. A follow-up study of discharged alcoholics. *Hospital and Community Psychiatry,* **21**: 94-94, 1970.

23. Pokorny, A.D., Miller, B.A., & Cleveland, S.E. Response to treatment of alcoholism: a follow-up study. *Quarterly Journal of Studies on Alcohol,* **29**: 364-381, 1968.

24. Feher, D. Psychotherapy. In R.E. Tarter and A.A. Superman (Eds.) *Alcoholism: Interdisciplinary Approaches to an Enduring Problem.* Reading, Massachusetts: Addison-Wesley, 1976.

25. Shaffer, J.B., & Galinsky, M.D. *Models of group therapy and sensitivity training.* Englewood Cliffs, New Jersey: Prentice-Hall, 1974.

26. Lieberman, M.A., Yalom, I.D. & Miles, M.B. *Encounter groups: first facts.* New York: Basic Books, 1973.

27. Rogers, C.R. *Client-centered therapy.* Boston: Houghton-Mufflin, 1951.

28. Rogers, Carl R. *On becoming a person.* Boston: Houghton-Mufflin, 1961.

29. Rogers, Carl R. *On becoming partners: Marriage and its alternatives.* New York: Delacorte, 1972.

30. Ellis, A. *Growth through reason: Verbatim cases in rational-emotive therapy.* Palo Alto, Cal.: Science and Behavior Books, 1971.

31. Ellis, A. *Humanistic Psychotherapy: the rational-emotive approach.* New York: Julian Press, 1973.

32. Ellis, A. *Reason and emotion in psychotherapy.* New York: Lyle Stuart, 1962.

33. Ellis, A., & Harper, R.A. *A guide to rational living.* Hollywood, Cal.: Wilshire, 1961.

34. Glasser, W. *Reality Therapy.* New York: Harper & Row, 1965.

35. Glasser, W. *Positive Addictions,* New York: Harper & Row, 1976.

36. Berne, Eric *Games People Play.* New York: Grove Press, 1964.

37. Berne, Eric *Transactional Analysis in Psychotherapy.* New York: Grove Press, 1961.

38. Harris, Thomas *I'm O.K. — You're O.K.* New York: Harper & Row, 1969.

39. Rimm, D.C., & Masters, J.C. *Behavior Therapy: Techniques and Empirical Findings.* New York: Academic Press, 1974.

40. Skinner, B.F. *Science and Human Behavior.* New York: Macmillan, 1953.

41. Wolpe, J. *Psychotherapy by Reciprocal Inhibition.* Stanford, Cal: Stanford University Press, 1958.

42. Lazarus, A.A. *Behavior therapy and beyond.* New York: McGraw-Hill, 1971.

43. Wolpe, J. *The practice of behavior therapy.* (2nd Ed.) New York: Pergamon, 1973.

44. Nathan, P.E. Alcoholism. In H. Leitenberg, (Ed.) *Handbook of behavior modification.* Englewood Cliffs, New Jersey: Prentice-Hall, 1976.

45. Miller, P.M. *Behavioral Treatment of Alcoholism.* New York: Pergamon, 1976.

46. Cautela, J.R. Covert sensitization. *Psychological Reports,* **20**: 459-468, 1967.

47. Cautela, J.R. The treatment of alcoholism by covert sensitization. *Psychotherapy: Theory, Research and Practice,* **7**: 86-90, 1970.

48. Smith-Moorhouse, P.M. Hypnosis in the treatment of alcoholism. *British Journal of Addictions,* **64**: 47-55, 1969.

49. Edwards, G. & Guthrie, S. A comparison of inpatient and outpatient treatment of alcohol dependence. *Lancet,* **1**: 467-468, 1966.

50. Rosenfeld, E.*The Book of Highs.*New York: Quadrangle/The New York Times Book Co., 1973.

51. Barber, T.X. *Hypnosis: A Scientific Approach.* New York: Van Nostrand Reinhold, 1969.

52. Cappell, H., & Herman, C.P. Alcohol and tension reduction: A Review. *Quarterly Journal of Studies on Alcohol,* **33:** 33-64, 1972.

53. Hamburg, S. Behavior therapy in alcoholism: A critical review of broad-spectrum approaches. *Journal of Studies on Alcohol,* **36:** 69-87, 1975.

54. Jacobson, E. *Progressive Relaxation.* Chicago: University of Chicago Press, 1938.

55. Bernstein, D.A., & Borkovec, T.D. *Progressive Relaxation Training: A Manual for the Helping Professions.* Champaign, Ill.: Research Press, 1973.

56. Walker, C.E. *Learn to Relax: 13 Ways to Reduce Tension.* Inglewood Cliffs, New Jersey: Prentice-Hall, 1975.

57. Benson, H. *The Relaxation Response.* New York: Avon, 1975.

58. Bloomfield, H.H., Cain, M.P., Jaffe, D.T., & Kory, R.B. *T.M.: Discovering Inner Energy and Overcoming Stress.* New York: Dell, 1975.

59. Hedberg, A.G., & Campbell, L.M. A comparison of four behavioral treatment approaches to alcoholism. *Journal of Behavior Therapy and Experimental Psychiatry,* **5:** 251-256, 1974.

60. Kraft, T. Social anxiety model of alcoholism. *Perceptual and Motor Skills,* **33:** 797-798, 1971.

61. Kraft, T., & Al-Issa, I. Alcoholism treated by desensitization: A case report. *Behaviour Research and Therapy,* **5:** 69-70, 1967.

62. Kraft, T., & Al-Issa, I. Desensitization and the treatment of alcoholic addiction. *British Journal of Addiction,* **63:** 19-23, 1968.

63. Lanyon, R.I., Primo, R.V., Terrell, F., & Wener, A. An aversion-desensitization treatment for alcoholism. *Journal of Consulting and Clinical Psychology,* **38:** 394-398, 1972.

64. Meichenbaum, D. Self-instructional methods. In F.H. Kanfer and A.P. Goldstein (Eds.), *Helping People Change.* New York: Pergamon, 1975.

65. Meichenbaum, D., & Cameron, R. The clinical potential of modifying what clients say to themselves. In M.J. Mahoney and C.E. Thoresen, (Eds.), *Self-control: Power to the person.* Monterey, Cal.: Brooks/Cole, 1974.

66. Lazarus, A., & Fay, A. *I Can If I Want To.* New York: Warner, 1975.

67. Marlatt, G.A. "A comparison of aversive conditioning procedures in the treatment of alcoholism." Paper presented at the annual meeting of the Western Psychological Association, Anaheim, Cal., 1973.

68. Marlatt, G.A., Kosturn, C.F. & Lang, A.R. Provocation to anger and opportunity for retaliation as determinants of alcohol consumption in social drinkers. *Journal of Abnormal Psychology,* **84:** 652-659, 1975.

69. Miller, P.M., Hersen, M., Eisler, R.M., & Hilsman, G. Effects of social stress on operant drinking of alcoholics and social drinkers. *Behavior Research and Therapy,* **12:** 67-72, 1974.

70. Eisler, R.M., Herson, M., Miller, P.M., & Blanchard, E.B. Situational determinants of assertive behaviors. *Journal of Consulting and Clinical Psychology,* **43:** 330-340, 1975.

71. Miller, P.M., Stanford, A.G., & Hemphill, D.P. A social-learning approach to alcoholism treatment. *Social Casework,* **55:** 279-284, 1974.

72. Vogler, R.E., Compton, J.V., & Weissbach, T.A. Integrated behavior change techniques for alcoholism. *Journal of Consulting and Clinical Psychology,* **43:** 233-243, 1975.

73. Eisler, R.M., Miller, P.M., Hersen, M., & Alford, H. Effects of assertive training on marital interaction. *Archives of General Psychiatry,* **30:** 643-649, 1974.

74. Rathus, S.A. A 30-item schedule for assessing assertive behavior. *Behavior Therapy,* **4:** 398-406, 1973.

75. Alberti, R.E., & Emmons, M.L. *Your Perfect Right* (2nd ed.), San Luis Obispo, Cal.: Impact, 1974.

76. Smith, M.J. *When I Say No, I Feel Guilty.* New York: Dial Press, 1975.

77. Phelps, S., & Austin, N. *The Assertive Woman.* San Luis Obispo, Cal.: Impact, 1975.
78. O'Leary, D.E., O'Leary, M.R. & Donovan, D.M. Social skill acquisition and psychosocial development of alcoholics: A review. *Addictive Behaviors,* **1:** 111-120, 1976.
79. Gordon, T. *Parent Effectiveness Training.* New York: Peter H. Wyden, 1970.
80. Knox, D., *Marriage Happiness: A Behavioral Approach to Counseling.* Champaign, Ill.: Research Press, 1971.
81. Gambrill, E.D., & Richey, C.A. *It's Up to You: Development of Assertive Social Skills.* Mill Brae, Cal.: Les Femmes, 1976.
82. Langer, E., & Dweck, C. *Personal Politics: The Psychology of Making It.* Englewood Cliffs, New Jersey: Prentice-Hall, 1973.
83. Bach, G.S., & Beutsch, R.M. *Pairing.* New York: Avon, 1970.
84. Bach, G.S., & Goldberg, H. *Creative Aggression.* New York: Avon, 1974.
85. Bach, G.S., & Wyden, P. *The Intimate Enemy.* New York: Avon, 1968.
86. Sulzer, E.S. Behavior modification in adult psychiatric patients. In L.P. Ullman and L. Krasner, (Eds.), *Case Studies in Behavior Modification.* New York: Holt, Rinehart & Winston, 1965.
87. Miller, P.M., Hersen, M., Eisler, R.M. & Watts, J.G. Contingent reinforcement of lowered blood/alcohol levels in an outpatient chronic alcoholic. *Behavior Research and Therapy,* **12:** 261-263, 1974.
88. Hunt, G.M., & Azrin, N.H. The community-reinforcement approach to alcoholism. *Behavior Research and Therapy,* **11:** 91-104, 1973.
89. Miller, P.M., Hersen, M., & Eisler, R.M. Relative effectiveness of instructions, agreements, and reinforcement in behavioral contracts with alcoholics. *Journal of Abnormal Psychology,* **83:** 548-553, 1974.
90. Stuart, R.B. Operant-interpersonal treatment for marital discord. *Journal of Consulting and Clinical Psychology,* **33:** 187-196, 1969.
91. Boudin, H. Contingency contracting with drug abusers in the natural environment. *International Journal of Addictions,* **12:** 1-10, 1977.
92. Polakow, R.L., & Doctor, R. Treatment of marijuana and barbiturate dependency by contingency contracting, *Journal of Behavior Therapy and Experimental Psychiatry,* **4:** 375-377, 1973.
93. Cautela, J.R., & Kastenbaum, R.A. A reinforcement survey schedule for use in therapy, training and research. *Psychological Reports,* **20:** 1115-1130, 1967.
94. Bellack, A.S., Rozencsky, R., and Schwartz, J. A comparison of two forms of self-monitoring in a behavioral weight reduction program. *Behavior Therapy,* **5:** 523-530, 1974.
95. Fuller, R.K., Bebb, H.T., Littell, A.S., Houser, H.B., & Witschi, J.C. Drinking practices recorded by a diary method. *Quarterly Journal of Studies on Alcohol,* **33:** 1106-1121, 1972.
96. Mahoney, M.J., & Thoresen, C.E. (Eds.) *Self-control: Power to the Person.* Monterey, Cal.: Brooks/Cole, 1974.
97. Annon, J.S. *Behavioral Treatment of Sexual Problems: Brief Therapy.* New York: Harper & Row, 1976.
98. Annon, J.S. *The Behavioral Treatment of Sexual Problems Volume 2: Intensive Therapy.* Honolulu, Hawaii: Enabling Systems, 1975.
99. McIntire, R.W. *Child Psychology: A Behavioral Approach to Everyday Problems.* Kalamazoo, Michigan: Behaviordelia, 1975.
100. Stuart, R.B., & Davis, B. *Slim Chance in a Fat World.* Champaign, Ill.: Research Press, 1972.
101. Gary, V., & Guthrie, D. The effect of jogging on physical fitness and self-concept in hospitalized alcoholics. *Quarterly Journal of Studies on Alcohol,* **33:** 1073-1078, 1972.
102. McCamy, J.C., & Presley, J. *Human Life Styling.* New York: Harper Colophon Books, 1975.
103. Williams, R. *Nutrition Against Disease.* New York: Pitman, 1971.
104. Register, V.D., Marsh, S.R., Thurston, C.T., Fields, B.J., Horning, M.C., Hardinge,

M.G., & Sanchez, A. Influence of nutrients on intake of alcohol. *Journal of the American Dietetic Association,* **61**: 159-162, 1972.
105. Cheraskin, E., & Ringsdorf, W.M. *Psychodietetics.* New York: Bantam, 1974.
106. Adams, J. *Drink To Your Health.* New York: Harper's Magazine Press, 1976.
107. Lewinsohn, P.M., & Libet, J. Pleasant events, activity schedules, and depressions. *Journal of Abnormal Psychology,* **79**: 291-295, 1972.
108. MacPhillamy, D., & Lewinsohn, P. *Pleasant Events Schedule.* Eugene, Oregon: University of Oregon, 1971. (For sale by Peter Lewinsohn, Psychology Clinic, University of Oregon, Eugene, Oregon, 97403).
109. Otto, H., & Mann, J., (Eds.) *Ways of Growth.* New York: Viking, 1968.
110. Sobell, M.B., & Sobell, L.C. Individualized behavior therapy for alcoholics. *Behavior Therapy,* **4**: 49-72, 1973..
111. Sobell, M.B., & Sobell, L.C. Second year treatment outcome of alcoholics treated by individualized behavior therapy: Results. *Behavior Research and Therapy,* **14**: 195-215, 1976.

CHAPTER 6

1. Hamburg, S. Behavior therapy in alcoholism: A critical review of broad-spectrum approaches. *Journal of Studies on Alcohol,* **36**: 69-87, 1975.
2. Moore, R. The diagnosis of alcoholism in a psychiatric hospital; a trial of the Michigan Alcoholism Screening Test (MAST). *American Journal of Psychiatry,* **128**: 1565-1569, 1972.
3. Selzer, M.L. The Michigan alcoholism screening test: the quest for a new diagnostic instrument. *American Journal of Psychiatry,* **127**: 1653-1658, 1971.
4. Lazarus, A.A. *Behavior therapy and beyond.* New York: McGraw-Hill, 1971.
5. Marlatt, G.A. The Drinking Profile: A questionnaire for the behavioral assessment of alcoholism. In E.J. Mash and L.G. Terdal, (eds.) *Behavior therapy assessment: Diagnosis, design and evaluation.* New York: Springer, 1976.
6. Shelton, J.L., & Ackerman, J.M. *Homework in Counseling and Psychotherapy.* Springfield, Ill.: Charles C. Thomas, 1974.
7. Sobell, M.B., & Sobell, L.C. A brief technical report on the MOBAT: an inexpensive portable test for determining blood alcohol concentration. *Journal of Applied Behavior Analysis,* **8**: 117-120, 1975.
8. Adams, J. *Drink to Your Health.* New York: Harper's Magazine Press, 1976.
9. Miller, W.R., & Munoz, R.F. *How to control your drinking.* Englewood Cliffs, New Jersey: Prentice-Hall, 1976.
10. Sobell, M.B., & Sobell, L.C. Individualized behavior therapy for alcoholics. *Behavior Therapy,* **4**: 49-72, 1973.
11. Kanfer, F.H., & Saslow, G. Behavioral diagnosis. In C.M. Franks, (Ed.), *Behavior therapy: Appraisal and status.* New York: McGraw-Hill, 1969.

CHAPTER 7

1. Sobell, M.B., and Sobell, L.C. Individualized behavior therapy for alcoholics. *Behavior Therapy,* **4**: 49-72, 1973.
2. Belasco, J.A., The criterion question revisited. *British Journal of Addiction,* **66**: 39-44, 1971.
3. Pattison, E.M. A critique of abstinence criteria in the treatment of alcoholism. *International Journal of Social Psychiatry,* **14**: 268-276, 1968.
4. Paul, G.C. Strategy of outcome research in psychotherapy. *Journal of Consulting Psychology,* **31**: 109-118, 1967.

5. Poley, W. and Mallett, L.S. *Personality and Social Adjustment Following Out-Patient Treatment for Alcoholism,* Alberta Alcoholism and Drug Abuse Commission, Research Report No. 2, Vol. 2, 1975.
6. Pattison, E.M. A critique of alcoholism treatment concepts; With special reference to abstinence. *Quarterly Journal of Studies on Alcohol,* **27:** 49-71, 1966.
7. Pattison, E.M., Headley, E.G., Gleser, G.C., and Gottschalk, L.A. Abstinence and normal drinking. *Quarterly Journal of Studies on Alcohol,* **29:** 610-633, 1968.
8. Baekeland, F., Lundwall, L., & Kissin, B. Methods for the treatment of chronic alcoholism: a critical appraisal. In R. Gibbins, Y. Israd, H. Kalant, R. Popham, W. Schmidt, and R. Smart (eds.) *Research Advances in Alcohol and Drug Problems: Volume Two.* New York: John Wiley & Sons, 1975.
9. Sobell, M.B., & Sobell, L.C. Second year treatment outcome of alcoholics treated by individualized behavior therapy: Results. *Behavior Research and Therapy,* **14:** 195-215, 1976.
10. Kiresuk, T., and Sherman, R. Goal attainment scaling: A general method for evaluating comprehensive community mental health programs. *Community Mental Health Journal,* **4:** 443-453, 1968.
11. Weinstein, M., and Ricks, F. Goal-attainment scaling: planning and outcome. *Canadian Journal of Behavioural Science,* **9:** 1-11, 1977.
12. Armor, D.J., Polich, J.M., and Stambul, H.B. *Alcoholism and Treatment: A Rand Corporation Research Study.* New York: John Wiley & Sons, Inc. 1978.

AUTHOR INDEX

M

McCamy, J.C., 83
McCord, J., 34
McCord, W., 34
McIntire, R.W., 83
Mallett, L.S., 128
Mann, J., 84
Marlatt, G.A., 77, 86
May, R., 38
Miles, M.B., 64
Miller, P.M., 52, 68, 80
Miller, W.R., 23, 52, 89
Munoz, R.F., 23, 89

N

Nathan, P.E., 68
Noble, E.P., 28
Norris, J., 49

O

Otto, H., 84

P

Perls, F., 35
Phelps, S., 79
Pinder, L. 59
Pokorny, A.D., 63
Poley, W., 37, 128, 130
Popham, R.E., 11
Presley, J., 83

R

Ranking, J.G., 11
Rathus, S.A., 78
Register, V.D., 83
Richey, C.A., 80
Ringsdorf, W.M., 83
Roe, A., 39
Rogers, C.R., 65
Rosenfeld, E., 70, 84

S

Sandor, S., 28
Schmidt, W., 11
Seely, J.R., 11
Shaffer, J.B., 64
Shelton, J.L., 87
Skinner, B.F., 67
Smart, R., 12
Smith, D.W., 27, 28
Smith, M.J., 79
Smith-Morehouse, P.M., 71
Sobell, M.B., 51, 130
Steffen, J.J., 63
Steiner, C., 66, 67
Stevens, T., 14, 15
Stuart, R.B., 82, 83

T

Thistle, R., 9
Tze, W.J., 28

V

Vibe, G., 9, 130
Victor, M., 46, 47

W

Walker, C.E., 72
Wanberg, K., 43
Westfield, D.R., 63
Williams, R.J., 40, 83
Wilsnack, S.C., 38
Winters, A., 50
Wolfe, S.M., 46
Wolff, K., 63
Wolpe, J., 67, 71, 75

Y

Yalom, I.D., 64

SUBJECT INDEX

A

Abusive drinking, assessing reasons for, 85-87, 121-123
  behavioral, 121
  etiological, 122-123
  personal, 121
  and treatment technique, 123
  see also Behavioral assessment; Client personal history; Continuous data; Michigan alcoholism screening test;
Adolescents, and alcohol consumption, 10, 12, 13
Alcohol, caloric value of, 24
  concentration of, in beverage, 17
  defined, 17
  distillation of, 17
  as drug, 1
  effects of, *see* Brain; Central nervous system; Cirrhosis; Heart disease; Hypoglycemia; Malnutrition; Medical effects; Pregnancy
  fermentation of, 17
  in history, 4
Alcohol Abuse and Alcoholism, National Institute of, 14
Alcohol abusers, number of, 12-13
Alcohol and alcoholism, further information on, 137-138
Alcohol and Alcoholism, National Institute on, 28
Alcohol and Health, First Special Report to the U.S. Congress on, 6, 12
Alcoholic, defined, 13
Alcoholics Anonymous (A.A.), 47-49, 53
  location of, 49
  meetings, function of, 47-48
  membership, composition of, 48-49
  membership, size of, 47
  philosophy of, 48
  Purpose of, 47
  success of, 49
  see also Industry

Antabuse (Disulfiram), use of in treatment, 61, 89
  effectiveness of, 61
  problems with, 61
  with other drugs, 62
Antidepressants and tranquilizers,
  abuse of, 61-62
  effectiveness of, 61
  use of in treatment, 61-62
Assertive training, as treatment technique, 76-79
  application of, 78-79
  defined, 76-77
  effectiveness of, 77
Assessment, of reasons for drinking, *see* Abusive drinking
Auto Accidents and fatalities, alcohol related, 30
Availability, of alcohol, and relation to alcoholism, 33-34, 40
Aversion therapy, as treatment technique, 68
  effectiveness of, 68
  see also Behavior therapy

B

Behavioral assessment, of alcohol abuse, 100-107
  and beverage preferences, 100-101
  defined, 86
  and drinking history, 102-105
  and effects of drinking, 101-102
  and emotional history, 105-106
  and reasons for, 105
  and sexual history, 106
Behavior therapy, defined, 67
  Controlled drinking and, 51, 52
  Drinkwatchers and, 50
  theory of, 67-68
  as treatment technique, 67--68, 128
  see also Aversion therapy; Covert sensitization
Biochemistry, and alcoholism, 40